Mastering Arabic 1

Activity Book

Practice for beginners

Second edition

Jane Wightwick &
Mahmoud Gaafar

HIPPOCRENE BOOKS, INC.
New York

Hippocrene Books, Inc. edition, 2015.

First published in English by Palgrave Macmillan, a division of Macmillan Publishers Limited under the title *Mastering Arabic 1 Activity Book, 2nd edition* by Jane Wightwick and Mahmoud Gaafar. This edition has been published under license from Palgrave Macmillan. The authors have asserted their right to be identified as the author of this Work.

ISBN 13: 978-0-7818-1339-6
ISBN 10: 0-7818-1339-5

First edition 2011
Second edition 2015

Cataloging-in-Publication data available from the Library of Congress.

For more information, contact:
HIPPOCRENE BOOKS, INC.
171 Madison Avenue
New York, NY 10016
www.hippocrenebooks.com

Printed in China.

Contents

Introduction

Practice, practice, practice!

The early stages of learning a new language are a steep learning curve, especially when you are also coping with an unfamiliar script, as you are with Arabic. If you want the language to stick in the long term, you really cannot have too much practice.

Mastering Arabic 1: Activity Book has been specifically developed to provide lively and enjoyable additional practice for beginners learning Arabic by themselves or within a group. The carefully graded activities will reinforce vocabulary and basic concepts in a variety of ways and so increase confidence and understanding of basic Arabic.

Mastering Arabic 1: Activity Book is especially suitable for use alongside the leading Arabic language course, *Mastering Arabic 1*. This new edition has been revised to complement the 20 units in the third (colour) edition of the main course. The vocabulary and structures used in *Mastering Arabic 1: Activity Book* are also taken directly from the main course and reworked to provide reinforcement. However, *Mastering Arabic 1: Activity Book* is also very useful for others beginning Arabic, and does not rely on knowledge of the main course.

The *Mastering Arabic* series teaches the universally understood Modern Standard Arabic. As in the main course, however, whenever there are dialogues or situations in which the colloquial language would naturally be used, we have tried to choose vocabulary and structures that are as close to the spoken form as possible. This approach has been chosen to help you understand Arabic in a variety of different situations.

How to use *Mastering Arabic 1: Activity Book*

You can use *Mastering Arabic 1: Activity Book* to reinforce your learning as you go along. The contents list on pages 3 and 4 indicates the main areas covered by the activities in each unit. Choose an activity that will help you practise what you are currently learning.

Alternatively, you can use *Mastering Arabic 1: Activity Book* to review the basics of the Arabic language before you move on to a higher level. The answers at the back of the book will help you to assess your progress. Try to revisit areas about which you feel uncertain. Then come back and try the activities again.

Mastering Arabic website

At www.palgrave.com/masteringarabic you will find a wealth of activities to help you with your studies, including audio flashcards, extra worksheets and videos.

Acknowledgements

We would like to thank Taoufiq Cherkaoui, Petros Samano and Najiba Keane, who reviewed the activities in this book. The encouragement and valuable comments provided by these experienced Arabic teachers have made an important contribution to the book. We are also very grateful for the continuing support of the team at Palgrave Macmillan, particularly Helen Bugler, Isobel Munday and Phillipa Davidson-Blake.

The authors and publisher would like to thank the following for permission to reproduce photographs: Fotalia.com: keko64, p52.

unit 1

Getting started

1 Match the Arabic script to the pronunciation, as in the example.

3	bu		tu
	tha		thi
	yu		ni
	ya		ti
	ba		na

1 بَ	6 يُ
2 تِ	7 ثَ
3 بُ	8 نِ
4 ثِ	9 تُ
5 نَ	10 يَ

Tip: From the start, accustom yourself to reading Arabic lists from top right to bottom left.

2 Write the vowel signs on these letters to match the pronunciation, as in the example.

1 nu نُ	5 yi ي
2 ta ت	6 tha ث
3 bi ب	7 bu ب
4 thu ث	8 tu ت

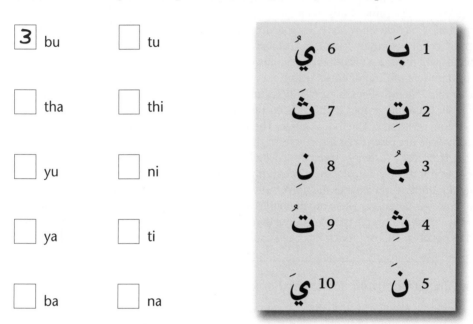

3 Complete the chart showing how each letter looks at the beginning, in the middle and at the end of a word.

←

At the end	In the middle	At the beginning	Letter
		بـ	(bā') ب
	ـتـ		(tā') ت
ـث			(thā') ث
		نـ	(nūn) ن
ـي			(yā') ي

4 How many of the Arabic letters above can you find in this news headline? Circle the letters as in the example, and then note below how many times each letter appears.

ثابت البنّا وزير التعليم اللبناني
في البيت الأبيض يوم الثلاثاء

ب ☐ ت ☐ ث ☐ ن ☐ ي ☐

5 Handwriting practice

بنت bint (girl/daughter)

بيت bayt (house)

بنّ bunn (coffee beans)

بين bayna (between)

تبن tibn (hay)

Tip: Add the dots on the letter shapes *after* completing the main shape of the word.

6 Choose the correct alternative for joining these letters, as in the example.

1 ن + ت + ب = a نيب (b) نتب c تبن

2 ب + ن + ي = a بني b بين c نبي

3 ي + ث + ب = a يتب b يثب c ثيب

4 ت + ن + ن = a نتن b تبّ c تنّ

5 ي + ن + ب + ت = a يبت b يبنت c ينبت

6 ت + ث + ب + ت = a يثبت b نثبت c تثبت

7 ب + ي + ي + ن = a بيّن b بينّ c بّين

8 ن + ب + ن + ي = a بنبي b نبني c بنّي

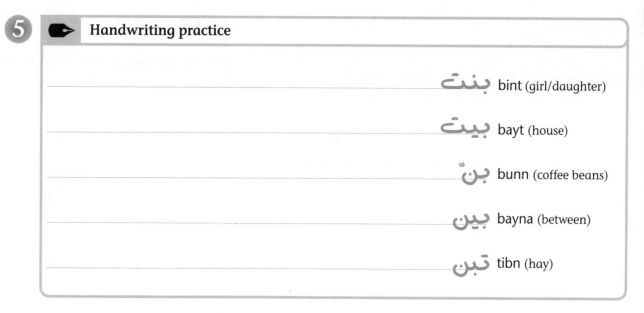

7 Arrange the letters and add the vowels to label the pictures, as in the example.

1 

ت ب ي

بَيت

2 

ن ب ت

______

3 

ن ب ي

______

4 

نّ ب

______

5 

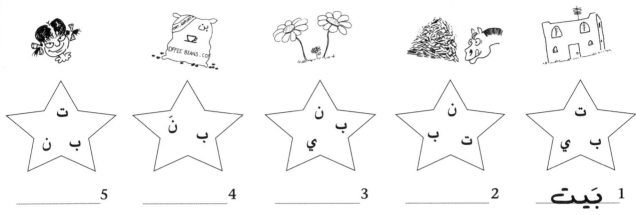

ت ب ن

______

8

Conversation

Practise replying to these greetings. Try saying your reply out loud.

You may not be familiar yet with all of the Arabic letters, so use the transliteration that follows to help you pronounce the words and write your response.

1 *(good morning)* صباح الخير ṣabāḥ al-khayr

______ *(reply)*

2 *(good evening)* مساء الخير masā' al-khayr

______ *(reply)*

3 *(hello)* أهلاً ahlan

______ *(reply to a male)*

4 *(hello)* أهلاً ahlan

______ *(reply to a female)*

unit 2

Putting words together

1 Eleven Arabic letters are hidden in this picture. Can you find them all?

2 Write the names by joining the letters, as in the example. (Take care to leave a small space after each of the six non-joining letters.)

1 ن + و + ر = نور

2 ز + ي + ن = ____

3 أ + ن + د + ي = ____

4 ب + ا + ر + ي = ____

5 ز + ي + د = ____

6 أ + ن + و + ر = ____

7 د + ا + ن + ي = ____

8 ن + ا + د + ر = ____

9 د + ي + ن + ا = ____

10 ث + ا + ب + ت = ____

3 Now join the two names together using و wa- ('and'), as in the example.

1 Dina/Nour دينا وَنور

2 Andy/Zayn ____

3 Anwar/Zayd ____

4 Thabit/Barry ____

5 Nour/Danny ____

6 Barry/Nadir ____

7 Anwar/Dina ____

8 Nadir/Andy ____

4 Handwriting practice

أنا anā (I)

أنتَ anta (you, *masc.*)

أنتِ anti (you, *fem.*)

و wa- (and)

وأنت؟ wa-anta/-i (and you?)

5 Choose the correct translation to match the speech bubble.

1 أنا زيد.

- **a** I'm Zayn.
- **b** I'm Zayd.
- **c** You're Zayd.

2 أنا زين وأنت؟

- **a** I'm Zayn, and you?
- **b** I'm Zaynab, and you?
- **c** Are you Zayn?

3 أنا أنور.

- **a** I'm Nur.
- **b** I'm Anwar.
- **c** I'm Adnan.

4 أنتَ دينو؟

- **a** Are you Dina?
- **b** Are you Danny?
- **c** Are you Dino?

5 أنت روزا.

- **a** You're Rosa.
- **b** You're Rose.
- **c** I'm Rose.

6 أنا بدر وأنت؟

- **a** I'm Brad, and you?
- **b** I'm Bart, and you?
- **c** I'm Badr, and you?

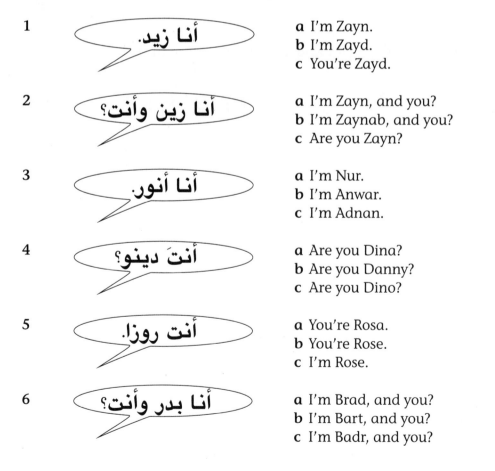

6 How do you say these in Arabic?

1 I'm Zayd. أنا زيد.

2 I'm Nour, and you *(fem.)*?

3 I'm Badr, and you *(masc.)*?

4 I'm Danny.

5 Are you Anwar?

6 Are you Zaynab?

7 **Conversation**

You have just bumped into a friend, Zaynab. She is with her brother, Anwar, whom you haven't met before.

Prepare your half of the conversation and try saying it out loud. As before, you can use the transliteration that follows the Arabic script to help you pronounce the words and write your response until you are familiar with all of the Arabic letters.

Use the English prompts to guide you, as in the example.

أنت: *Hello, Zaynab.* أهلاً يا زينب. ahlan yā zaynab.

زينب: أهلاً بك. ahlan bik(a)/biki.

أنت: *How are you?*

زينب: الحمد الله. al-ḥamdu lillāh.

أنت: *Are you Anwar?*

أنور: نعم، أنا اسمي أنور. naɛam *(yes)*, anā ismī anwar.

أنت: *Pleased to meet you, Anwar.*

أنور: تشرّفنا. tasharrafnā.

unit

3 The family

1 Match the letter combinations to their joined-up equivalents.

a	حامد	1	م + ه + ا
b	ماري	2	ح + ا + م + د
c	حاتم	3	ه + ا + ن + ي
d	مها	4	ح + ا + ت + م
e	ياسمين	5	م + ا + ر + ي
f	هاني	6	ي + ا + س + م + ي + ن

2 **Handwriting practice**

هذا hādha (this, *masc.*)

هذه hādhihi (this, *fem.*)

زجاجة zujāja (bottle)

خيمة khayma (tent)

أحمد aḥmad (Ahmed)

هو huwa (he)

هي hiya (she)

Tip: The letter hā' (ه) needs special attention. The letter shape varies considerably, depending on its position, and hā' also has an alternative shape in the middle (ـهـ or ـهـ).

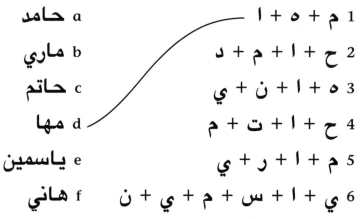

3 Look at the pictures and find each word in the word square. (The words can be found running right to left or top to bottom.) Then write the Arabic (joined up) next to the picture and decide whether the word is masculine (M) or feminine (F), as in the example.

ث	ا	ذ	د	ت	ي	ب
ة	ر	خ	م	ر	ه	ن
ج	ب	ي	ت	ي	ذ	ت
ر	ا	م	ح	ذ	ث	ر
ي	ث	ة	ج	ا	ج	د
د	ا	م	ح	ب	م	ه
ة	ج	ا	ج	ز	ي	ذ

1  زُجاجة ______ [F]

2  ______ [ ]

3  ______ [ ]

4  ______ [ ]

5  ______ [ ]

6  ______ [ ]

7  ______ [ ]

8  ______ [ ]

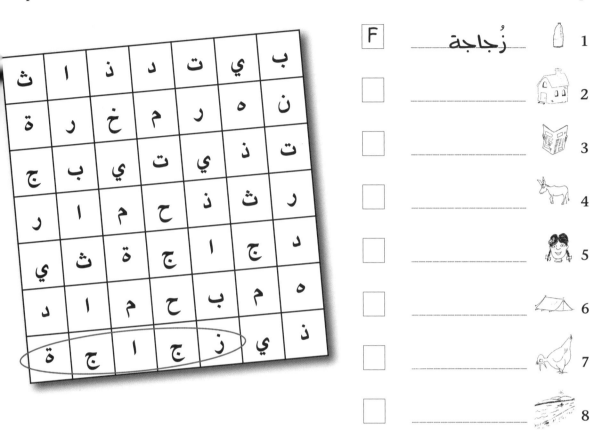

4 Rewrite the words below, adding the ending ي -ī ('my'), as in the example.

1 أَخ (brother) ⟵ أخي (my brother)

2 أَب (father) ⟵ ______

3 أُمّ (mother) ⟵ ______

4 أُخت (sister) ⟵ ______

5 إِبن (son) ⟵ ______

6 بِنت (daughter) ⟵ ______

7 زَوج (husband) ⟵ ______

8 زَوجة (wife) ⟵ ______

9 بَيت (house) ⟵ ______

10 مَدينة (city/town) ⟵ ______

Tip: When you add the ending, adjust the final letter to the joining shape and remember that the feminine ending tā' marbūṭa (ة) is then written and pronounced as a regular tā' (ـتـ).

5 Complete the names of the family members on the family trees below, according to what the people are saying. (*Note:* '=' means 'married to')

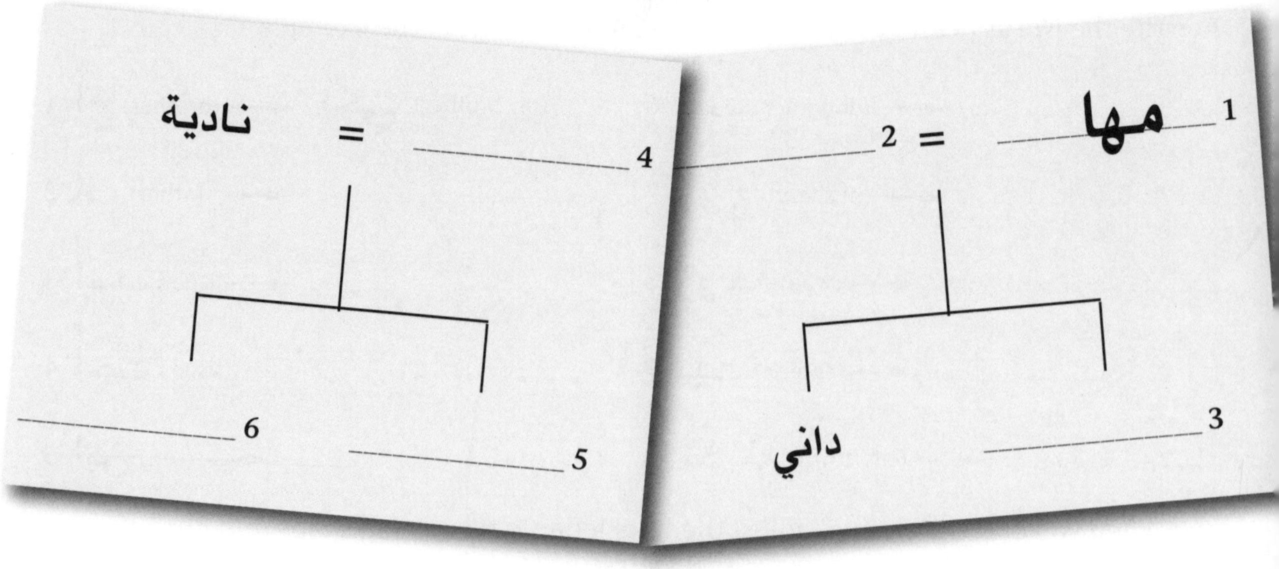

6 How do you say these in Arabic?

1 This is my husband, Hamed. هذا زوجي، حامد.

2 This is my mother, Maha. ______

3 Mary is Ayman's daughter. ______

4 Nadia is Hamed's wife. ______

5 Who's Badr? He's my son. ______

6 Who's Mary? She's my daughter. ______

7

Conversation

Your father and your little sister are seeing you off at the train station when you bump into your friend Zaynab again. (*Note:* train = قطار qiṭār)

Prepare your half of the conversation, introducing your father and sister to Zaynab, and try saying it out loud. Remember that you can use the transliteration to help you pronounce the words and write your response; but you may also now want to have a go at writing some of the words in Arabic script.

Use the English prompts to guide you, as in the example.

زينب: أهلاً. ahlan.

أنت: *How are you, Zaynab?* كيف الحال يا زينب؟ kayf al-ḥāl yā zaynab?

زينب: الحمد لله al-ḥamdu lillāh.

أنت: *Zaynab, this is my father.* ______

زينب: تشرّفنا. ومن هذه؟ tasharrafnā. wa-man hādhihi?

أنت: *This is my sister, Mimi.* ______

زينب: أهلاً يا ميمي! ahlan yā mīmī!

أنت: *Ah, this is my train.* ______

زينب: مع السلامة! maɛa s-salāma!

أنت: *Goodbye!* ______

unit 4 Jobs

1 Complete the chart showing how these letters look at the beginning, in the middle and at the end of a word.

At the end	In the middle	At the beginning	Letter
		ســ	(sīn) س
	ـشـ		(shīn) ش
		صـ	(ṣād) ص
ـض			(ḍād) ض

2 **Handwriting practice**

باص bāṣ (bus)

شورت shūrt (shorts)

سينما sīnimā (cinema)

مدرّس mudarris (teacher)

محاسب muḥāsib (accountant)

ممرّضة mumariḍḍa (nurse)

3 Match the members of the football team with their Arabic names, as in the example.

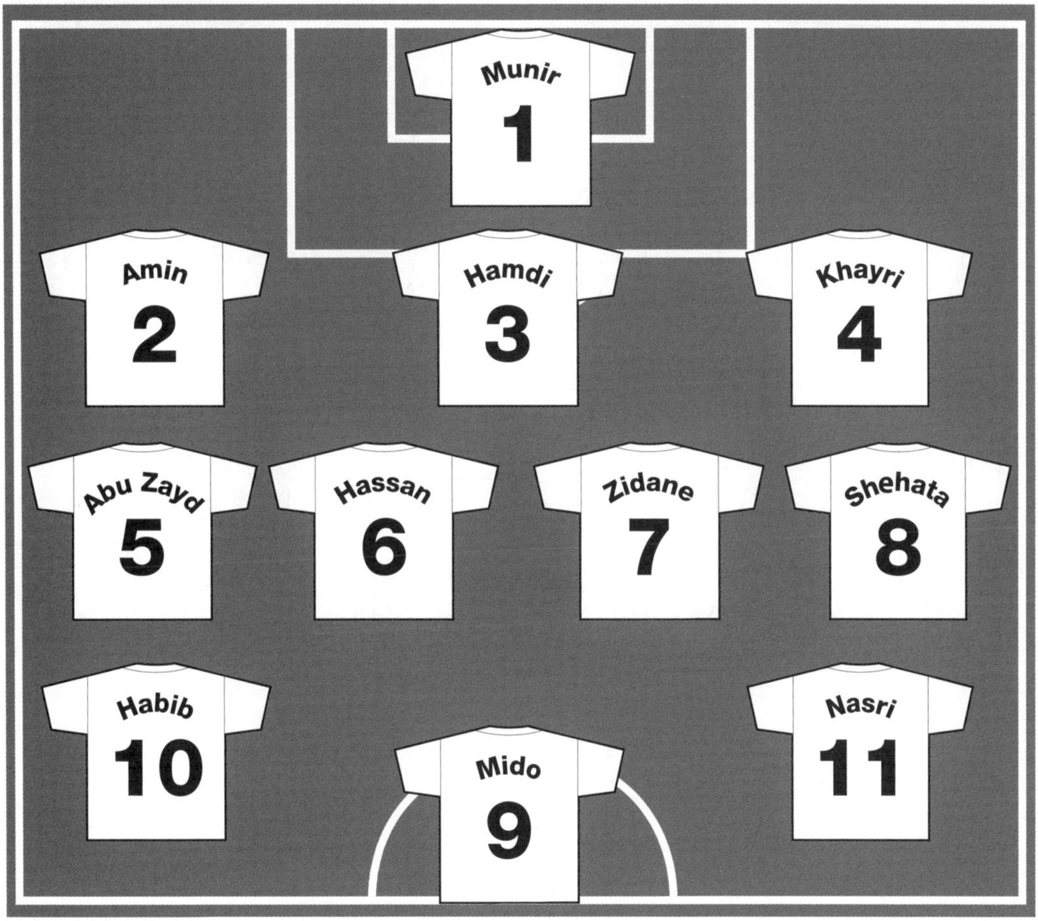

زيدان	7	أمين	☐
ميدو	☐	منير	☐
حبيب	☐	خيري	☐
شحاتة	☐	حمدي	☐
نصري	☐	أبو زيد	☐
حسن	☐		

4 Read what Sara tells you about her family in the picture and complete the table below.

أنا سارة وأنا مُدرّسة. هذا زوجي، حَسَن. هو مُصَوِّر.

هذه بنتي ياسمين، وهي مُحاسبة. وابني أمين، مُهندس.

وهذه هي أُمّي سميرة بَينَ ياسمين وأمين. أُمّي ممرّضة.

Name	Relationship to Sara	Job
Sara	——	teacher

5 Make the sentences plural, as in the example.

1 هو نجّار. — هم نجّارون . (They're carpenters.)

2 هو خبّاز. ______

3 أنا مهندس. ______

4 هي مدرّسة. ______

5 أنا محاسبة. ______

6 هو مصوّر. ______

7 هي مهندسة. ______

8 هي ممرّضة. ______

6 **Conversation**

You are talking to Sara about jobs, and what your families do for a living.
Prepare your half of the conversation and try saying it out loud.
Use the English prompts to guide you, as in the example.

أنت: *What's your job, Sara?* ما عملِك يا سارة؟ mā ʿamalik yā sāra?

سارة: أنا مدرّسة. وأنت؟ anā mudarrisa. w-anta(-i)?

أنت: *I'm a student. My father is a baker.* ______

سارة: آه! أنا أخي خبّاز! āh! anā akhī khabbāz!

أنت: *What's your husband's job?* ______

سارة: هو مصوّر. huwa muṣawwir.

أنت: *And your son and your daughter?* ______

سارة: أمين مهندس وياسمين محاسبة. amīn muhandis wa-yāsmīn muḥāsiba.

أنت: *Wonderful!* ______

unit 5

Describing things

1 Match the letter combinations to their joined-up equivalents.

1	م + ل + ف	a	قام
2	ق + ا + م	b	كاف
3	ك + ف + ل	c	ملف
4	ق + ل + م	d	قلم
5	ف + ل + ك	e	كفل
6	ك + ا + ف	f	فلك

2 **Handwriting practice**

- كلب kalb (dog)
- قلم qalam (pen)
- مكسور maksūr (broken)
- خفيف khafīf (light)
- ممكن؟ mumkin? (may I?)
- تفضّل tafaḍḍal (here you are)
- شكراً shukran (thank you)

Tip: You may find it helps the flow of your writing to add any dots on the letter shapes and the top stroke of the kaaf (ك) *after* completing the main shape of the word.

3 Arrange the letters and add the vowels to label the pictures, as in the example:

5 _____	4 _____	3 _____	2 _____	1 _____ قَلَم

ي م ق ص	ة ي خ م	ب ت ك ا	رَّ ا ة ج د	م ق ل

10 _____	9 _____	8 _____	7 _____	6 _____

ي ب ة ح ق	ك ل ب	ف م ح ت ا	ا م خ ت	ا يَّ ر س ة

4 **هذه** or **هذا**؟
Write each word from Activity 3 in the correct column, as in the example.

هذه...	هذا...
	هذا قلم.

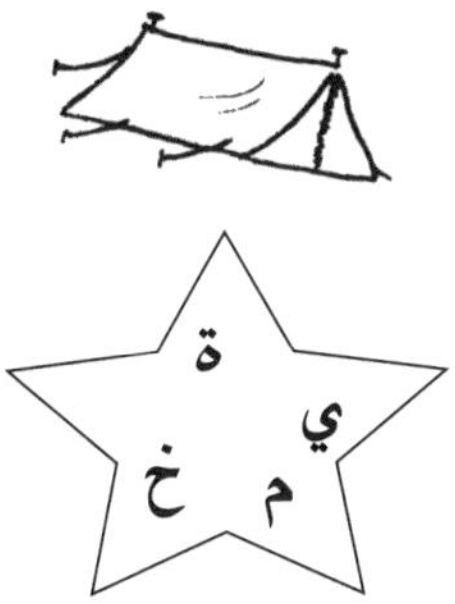

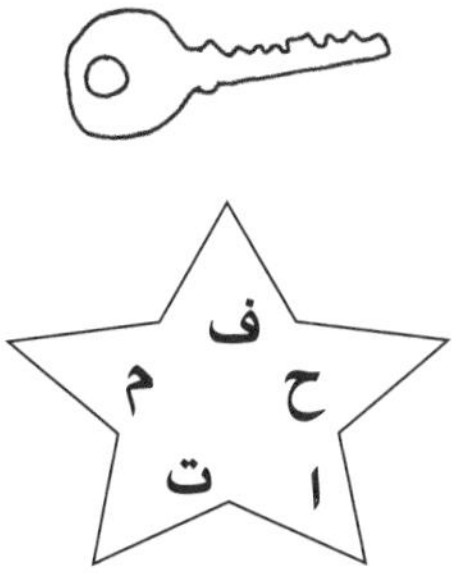

5 True or false? Look at the picture of Warda and decide which sentences are true.

1 زجاجة وردة مكسورة. ✔

2 درّاجة وردة جديدة.

3 شورت وردة أسود...

4 ...وقميصها أبيض.

5 خيمة وردة سليمة.

6 كتاب وردة ثقيل...

7 ...وهو كتاب أَسوَد.

8 خاتم وردة جميل.

6 Change 'a' to 'the' by adding ...ال (al-), as in the example .

1 بيت (a house) ⟵ البيت (the house) ____________

2 ولد (a boy) ⟵ ____________

3 نهر (a river) ⟵ ____________

4 زجاجة (a bottle) ⟵ ____________

5 مفتاح (a key) ⟵ ____________

6 جريدة (a newspaper) ⟵ ____________

7 تلميذ (a pupil) ⟵ ____________

8 قلم (a pen) ⟵ ____________

9 مدينة (a city) ⟵ ____________

10 خبّاز (a baker) ⟵ ____________

7 **Conversation**

You are in an Arabic-speaking country and need to write a quick shopping list.
You don't have a pen but you've noticed some for sale on a nearby newspaper stand.
Prepare your half of the conversation with the seller (البائع al-bā'iع) and try saying it out loud.
Use the English prompts to guide you, as in the example.

أنت: *Good morning* صباح الخير. ṣabāḥ al-khayr. ____________

البائع: صباح النور. ṣabāḥ an-nūr

أنت: *May I have (*ممكن mumkin*) a pen, please?* ____________

البائع: هذا القلم؟ hādhā l-qalam?

أنت: *No. I'd like the black [one].* ____________

البائع: تَفَضَّل(ي). tafaḍḍal(ī).

أنت: *This pen is broken!* ____________

البائع: آه! تَفَضَّل(ي). هذا القلم سليم. ah! tafaḍḍal(ī). hādhā l-qalam salīm.

أنت: *Thank you.* ____________

البائع: مع السلامة. maعa s-salāma.

أنت: *Goodbye.* ____________

unit 6

Where is it?

1 Complete the chart showing how each letter looks at the beginning, in the middle and at the end of a word.

At the end	In the middle	At the beginning	Letter
		طـ	(ṭā') ط
ـظ			(ẓā') ظ
	ـعـ		(ع ayn) ع
		غـ	(ghayn) غ

Tip: The letters ع ayn (ع) and ghayn (غ) change their shape significantly when they join.

2 Choose one of the letters in the table above to complete the word according to the English in brackets, as in the example.

1 عـرب (Arabs)

2 ☐ـالب (student)

3 ☐ـمل (work)

4 ☐ـزّة (Gaza)

5 ☐ـنجة (Tangiers)

6 بـ☐ـداد (Baghdad)

7 ☐ـنـ☐ـاء (Sanaa)

8 أبو ☐ـبي (Abu Dhabi)

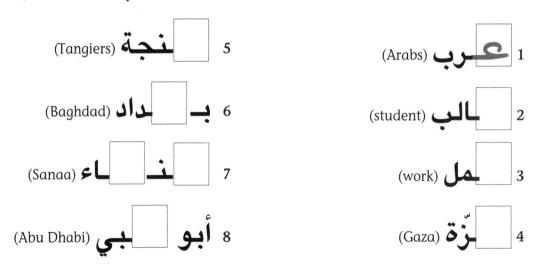

3 Match where the ball is in each picture to the correct positional word.

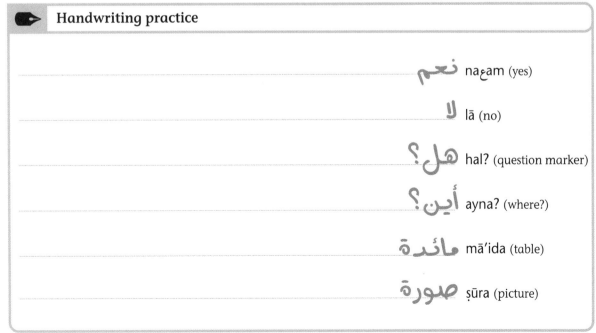

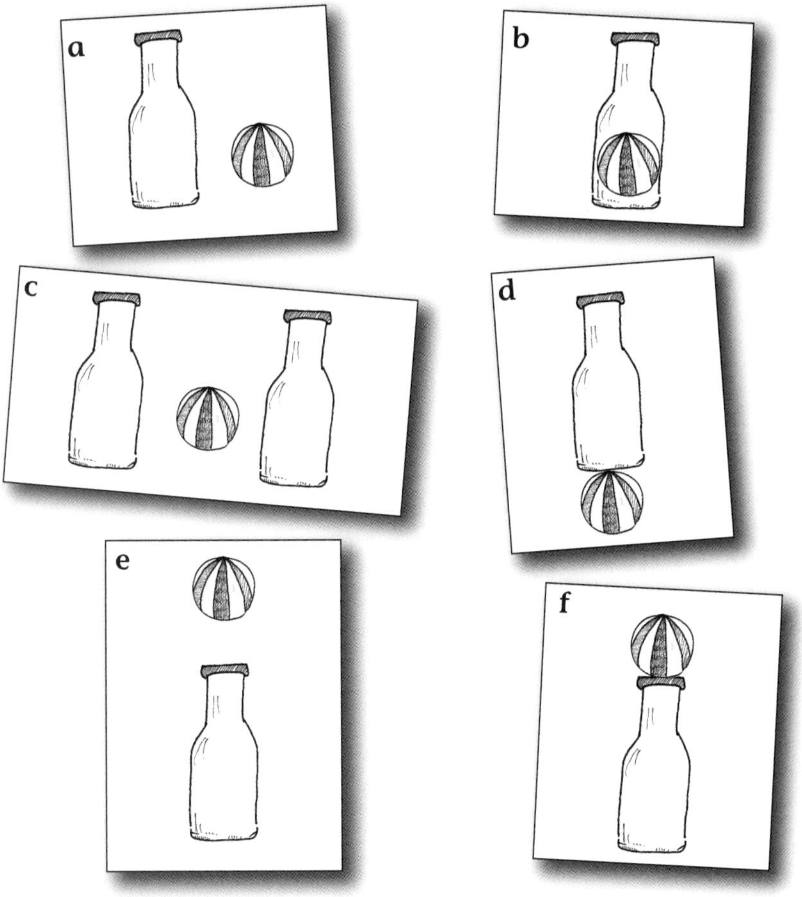

1 فوق

2 على

3 بجانب

4 بين

5 في

6 تحت

4 **Handwriting practice**

نعم naعam (yes)

لا lā (no)

هل؟ hal? (question marker)

أين؟ ayna? (where?)

مائدة mā'ida (table)

صورة ṣūra (picture)

5 Make sentences or questions from the picture prompts, as in the example.

1  تحت  . الخاتم تحت الكرسيّ.

2  في  . ____________

3 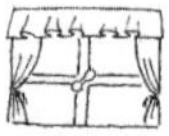 فوق 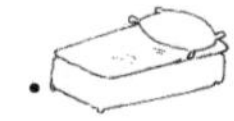 . ____________

4  في  ؟ ____________

5  على  ؟ ____________

6  بجانب  . ____________

7 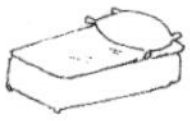 بين  و  . ____________

8  بين  و  ؟ ____________

6 In Arabic, try to describe the position of some items you see in the room you are currently using, or one you can easily visualise. Use your sentences above as models.

7 Write questions using the prompts, as in the example.

هل هذا سرير؟ ⟵ (bed) سَرير 1

⟵ (window) شُبّاك 2

⟵ (picture) صورة 3

⟵ (door) باب 4

⟵ (television) تليفزيون 5

⟵ (cupboard) خَزانة 6

⟵ (boat) مَركَب 7

⟵ (table) مائِدة 8

8 **Conversation**

You have found an interesting restaurant, and are asking the maitre d' (المتر) about a table. Prepare your half of the conversation and try saying it out loud. You should be able to have a go at writing your part. Use the English prompts to guide you, as in the example.

أنت: *Good evening.* مساء الخير. masā' al-khayr.

المتر: مساء النور. أهلاً وسهلاً. masā' an-nūr. ahlan wa-sahlan.

أنت: *I'd like a table, please.*

المتر: نعم. تَفَضَّل(ي). هذه المائدة؟ naعam. tafaḍḍal(ī). hādhihi l-mā'ida?

أنت: *No. I'd like a table beside the window, please.*

المتر: نعم. هذه المائدة؟ naعam. hādhihi l-mā'ida?

أنت: *Yes, the table under the picture.*

المتر: نعم. تَفَضَّل(ي). naعam. tafaḍḍal(ī).

أنت: *Lovely ['Beautiful']. Thank you!*

unit 7 Describing places

1 **Handwriting practice**

مدينة madīna (town)

غرفة ghurfa (room)

بنك bank (bank)

مدرسة madrasa (school)

مصنع maṣnaع (factory)

شارع shāriع (street)

مستشفى mustashfā (hospital)

2 How do you say these in Arabic?

1 a small factory مصنع صغير

2 the small factory

3 a big town

4 the big town

5 my new shirt

6 his big black dog

7 He's strong.

8 She's a tall girl.

3 Yusuf is on a student exchange and has written an email to his mother. Read the email and answer the questions in English.

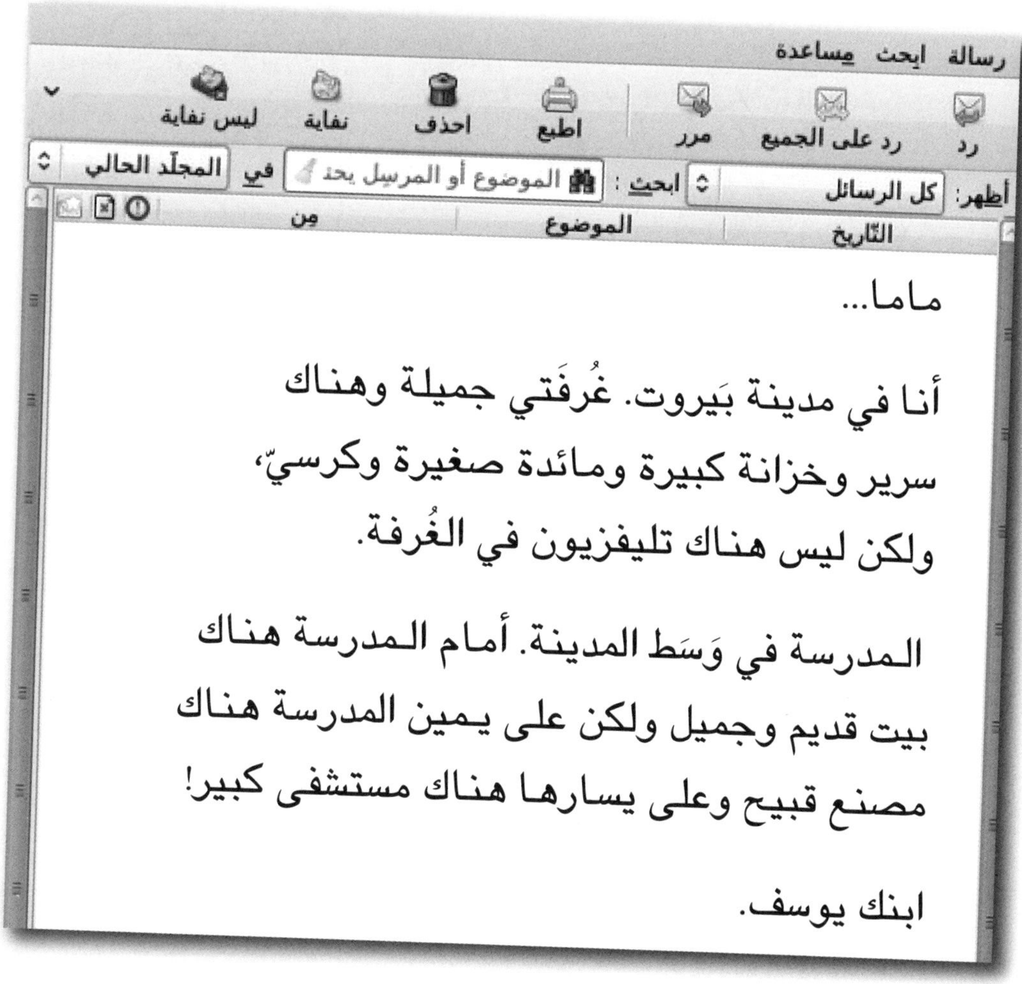

ماما...

أنا في مدينة بَيروت. غُرفَتي جميلة وهناك سرير وخزانة كبيرة ومائدة صغيرة وكرسيّ، ولكن ليس هناك تليفزيون في الغُرفة.

المدرسة في وَسَط المدينة. أمام المدرسة هناك بيت قديم وجميل ولكن على يمين المدرسة هناك مصنع قبيح وعلى يسارها هناك مستشفى كبير!

ابنك يوسف.

1 Which city is Yusuf visiting?

2 Does he like his room?

3 Is the cupboard big or small?

4 Are there a table and a chair in the room?

5 Is there a television?

6 Where is the school?

7 What is there in front of the school?

8 What two other buildings does Yusuf mention?

9 Which of these buildings is to the left of the school?

10 How does he sign off?

4 Mark the correct column depending on whether or not you can see the item in the picture, as in the example.

	هناك...	ليس هناك...
1 سيّارة		✘
2 مركب		
3 بنت		
4 ولد		
5 كتاب		
6 قلم		
7 باب		
8 كلب		
9 مائدة		

	هناك...	ليس هناك...
10 كرسيّ		
11 حمامة		
12 تينة		
13 دجاجة		
14 زجاجة		
15 شجرة		
16 درّاجة		
17 وردة		
18 ذبابة		

5 Now complete this description of the picture on page 32. (*Note:* أو aw = or)

في هذه الصورة هناك شجرة كبيرة. ________ الشجرة هناك

________ ثقيلة وكرسيّ. بجانب الكرسيّ هناك ________ صغيرة.

في وسط الصورة هناك ________ وهو على ________ .

________ الولد هناك بنت. كلب البنت أسود و ________ .

________ المائدة هناك زجاجة كولا ووردة ولكن ________

هناك قلم أو ________ .

6 **Conversation**

You are in a small Arabic-speaking town and you need to withdraw some money. You're not sure how to get to the bank, so you stop a man (رَجُل rajul) on the street to ask.

Prepare your half of the conversation and try saying it out loud as usual.

Use the English prompts to guide you, as in the example.

أنت: *Good morning.* صباح الخير. ṣabāḥ al-khayr. ________

الرجل: صباح النور. ṣabāḥ an-nūr

أنت: *How do I get to the bank, please?* ________

الرجل: خد ثاني شارع على اليسار. khud thāni shāriع ع‍alā l-yasār.

أنت: *Is the bank near to the school?* ________

الرجل: نعم. بجانب المدرسة. naعam. bijānib al-madrasa.

أنت: *Thank you. Goodbye.* ________

الرجل: مع السلامة. maعa s-salāma.

unit 8 Review

1 Complete the Arabic alphabet table and note whether the letter is a sun or a moon letter.

Sun/moon letter	Arabic script	Name of letter
		ḍād
		ṭā'
		ẓā'
		ع ayn
		ghayn
		fā'
		qāf
		kāf
		lām
		mīm
		nūn
		hā'
		wāw
		yā'

Sun/moon letter	Arabic script	Name of letter
moon	ا	alif
		bā'
		tā'
		thā'
		jīm
		ḥā'
		khā'
		dāl
		dhāl
		rā'
		zāy
		sīn
		shīn
		ṣād

Tip: Sun letters assimilate (take over) the 'l' sound when al- ('the') is added. Sun letters tend to be pronounced at the front of the mouth and/or with the teeth, while moon letters are those sounded further back in the mouth and do not affect the pronunciation of al-.

2 Look at the picture clues and complete the crossword. Remember that Arabic crosswords are compiled using the separate form of each letter. One clue is completed for you.

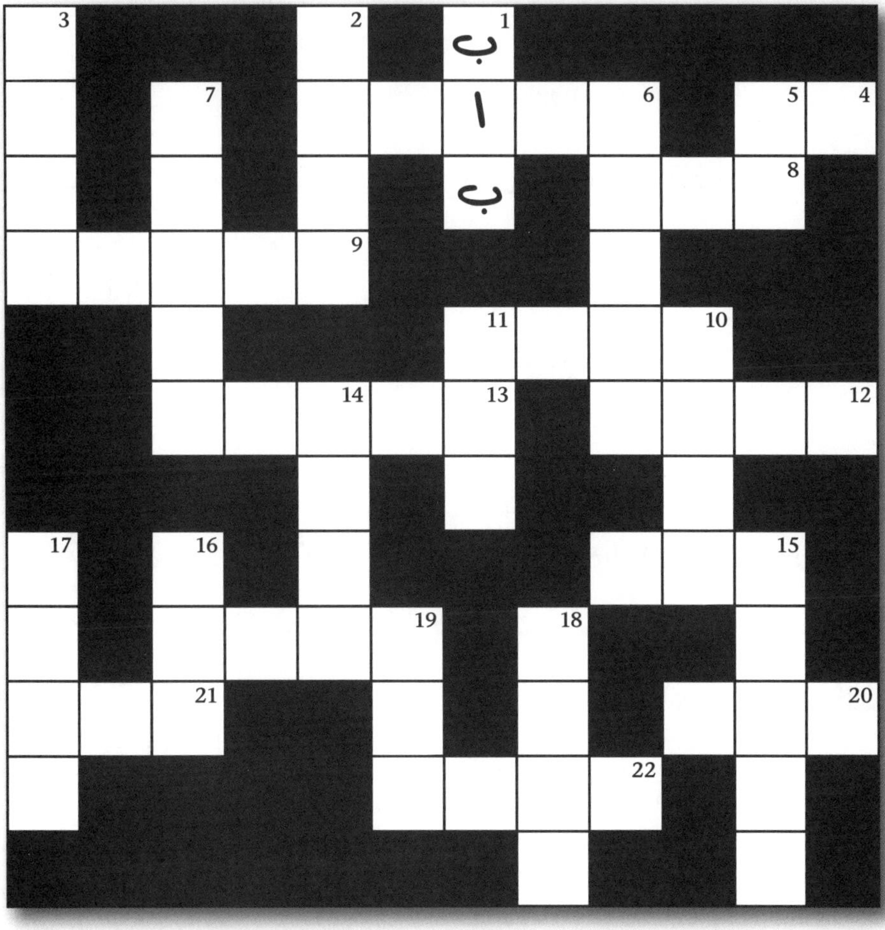

أُفقيّ ←

رأسيّ ↓

3 Rewrite the words below, using the appropriate possessive endings, as in the example.

1 بيت (her) ⟶ بيتها (her house)
2 أَب (my) ⟶ ____________
3 كتاب (his) ⟶ ____________
4 غُرفة (my) ⟶ ____________
5 اِبن (your *masc.*) ⟶ ____________
6 درّاجة (your *fem.*) ⟶ ____________
7 زَوج (her) ⟶ ____________
8 مَدرَسة (our) ⟶ ____________
9 مَدينة (their *masc.*) ⟶ ____________
10 سيّارة (their *masc.*) ⟶ ____________

4 Read the description of Karim and decide whether the sentences are true or false.

كريم طالِب في المَدرَسة. أبو كريم مُهندِس
وأمّه مُمرّضة. بَيتهم في وَسط المدينة بِجانب
المدرسة. هناك شَجَر جَميل أمام البيت.

البيت كبير ولكنّ غُرفة كريم صغيرة.
في غرفته هُناكَ سرير تحت الشبّاك
وخَزانة صَغيرة ومائدة. فوق المائدة
هناك تليفزيون ولكن ليس هناك كتاب!

	True	False
1 Karim is a school teacher.	❑	❑
2 His father is an accountant.	❑	❑
3 His mother is a nurse.	❑	❑
4 Their house is in the centre of town.	❑	❑
5 The house is small.	❑	❑
6 Karim's room is small.	❑	❑
7 There isn't a window in Karim's room.	❑	❑
8 There's a table in his room.	❑	❑
9 There's a television on the table.	❑	❑
10 Karim has lots of books.	❑	❑

5 How do you say these in Arabic?

1 The newspaper is under the chair. الجريدة تحت الكرسيّ.

2 There's a dog in the room. ______

3 There isn't a school in this town. ______

4 Is your *(masc.)* house big? ______

5 This is Zayn's bag. ______

6 Where's my mother? She's in the bank. ______

6

Conversation

You have made a reservation at a hotel and have now arrived at reception.

Prepare your half of the conversation with the hotel employee (المُوَظَّف) and try saying it out loud. Remember you can use the transliteration that follows the Arabic to help you pronounce and write your answers, but you may now also want to have a go at writing some of it in Arabic script.

Use the English prompts to guide you, as in the example. (*Note*: internet = إنترنت)

الموظّف: أهلاً. الاسم من فضلك. ahlan. al-ism min faḍlak.

أنت: *My name is Tom Lewis.* ismī Tom Lewis. اسمي توم لويس.

الموظّف: لويس... نعم. هذا هو المفتاح. Lewis..., naعam. hādhā huwa l-miftāḥ.

أنت: *Thank you. Where's my room?* ______

الموظّف: فوق الكافيتريا. fawqa l-kāfītiryā.

أنت: *My bag is in the car. The bag is heavy!* ______

الموظّف: أحمد! الحقيبة من فضلك! aḥmad! al-ḥaqība min faḍlak!

أنت: *And is there internet in the room?* ______

الموظّف: نعم يا سيّد لويس. naعam yā sayyid Lewis.

أنت: *Thank you.* ______

unit 9 Countries and people

1 Match the capital cities to the countries, as in the example.

a	بَغداد	1	مِصر
b	عَمّان	2	السودان
c	الرِّياض	3	عُمان
d	القاهِرة	4	ليبيا
e	الخَرطوم	5	اليَمَن
f	دِمَشق	6	العِراق
g	بَيروت	7	سوريا
h	صَنعاء	8	السَّعوديّة
i	مَسقَط	9	لُبنان
j	طَرابلُس	10	الأُردُنّ

2 Now describe the positions of the cities using the prompts, as in the example.

1 عمّان/شمال ← عمّان في شمال الأردنّ. (Amman is in the north of Jordan.)

2 طرابلس/غَرب ← ……………………

3 نيو يورك/شَرق ← ……………………

4 لُندن/جَنوب ← ……………………

5 بيروت/غرب ← ……………………

6 your [nearest] city ← ……………………

3 Fill in the chart below with the personal information about these five people.

Name	Nationality	Home town
Tom	English	Oxford

4 Describe the nationalities of the following people, as in the example.

1 جاك من باريس. (Jacques is from Paris) هو فرنسيّ. (He's French.) ______

2 حُسَين من بغداد. ______

3 نادية من دمشق. ______

4 هذا الطالب من روما. ______

5 هذه البنت من الخرطوم. ______

6 المهندسون من القاهرة. ______

7 المصوّرون من لُندُن. ______

8 المدرّسات من طوكيو. ______

5 Complete the gaps in the paragraph about Jacques, using the words in the box. You may only use each word once. The first gap has been completed as an example.

وسط	مصوّرة	البنك	أمّ	لبنان	~~فرنسيّ~~	مستشفى	من	في	جنوب

جاك فرنسيّ من باريس. أبو جاك ______

تولوز في ______ فرنسا ولكن أُمّه من بيروت

في ______. جاك محاسب في ______

اللبنانيّ في ______ المدينة. أبو جاك مهندس

______ مصنع صغير وأُخته

في جريدة لُبنانيّة. ______ جاك ممرّضة

في ______ بجانب بَيتهم.

6 Try to describe where you and your family come from and what they do, using the paragraph in Activity 5 as a model. You can talk about yourself, your mother and father, your siblings, your partner or your children.

7 **Conversation**

You are talking to Sara about where you are from. Prepare your half of the conversation and try saying it out loud. Use the English prompts to guide you, as in the example.

When you've finished, you can try the conversation again, this time substituting your own details.

أنت: *Where are you from, Sara?* أنتِ من أين يا سارة؟ anti min ayna yā sāra?

سارة: أنا عراقيّة من البصرة. وأنت؟ anā ɛirāqīyya min al-baṣra. w-anta(-i)?

أنت: *I'm English ...*

... but my mother is American.

سارة: أنت من أيّة مدينة؟ anta(-i) min ayyat madīna?

أنت: *I'm from Leeds.*

سارة: أين هذه المدينة؟ ayna hādhihi l-madīna?

أنت: *It's in the north of England.*

سارة: هل ليدز صغيرة؟ hal Leeds ṣaghīra?

أنت: *No. It's a big town.*

unit 10

Counting things

1 Write the Arabic figure next to the number; then put them in order, from the lowest to the highest.

a سِتّة [٦]
b ثَلاثة [ ]
c واحِد [ ]
d سَبعة [ ]
e أربَعة [ ]
f عَشَرة [ ]
g اِثنان [ ]
h تِسعة [ ]
i ثَمانية [ ]
j خَمسة [ ]

2 بِكَم؟ *(How much?)* Decide how much money there is, as in the example.

١  أربعة جنيهات

٢  ______________

٣ 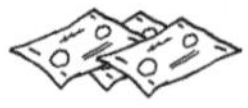 ______________

٤ 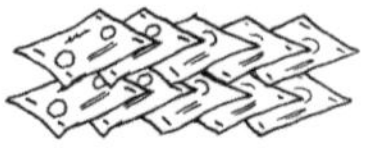 ______________

٥  ______________

٦  ______________

٧ 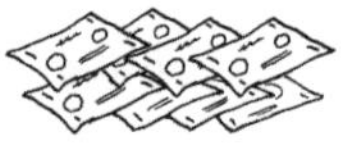 ______________

٨ 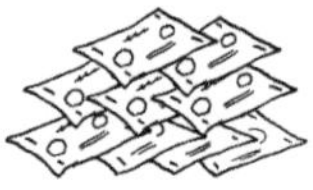 ______________

3 Arrange the letters to label these pictures of things you can buy in the market, as in the example.

١ و م ز — موز
٢ فّ ا ت ح — ____
٣ ن ل د ص — ____
٤ ق ب ط — ____
٥ ي ت ر ي ش ت — ____

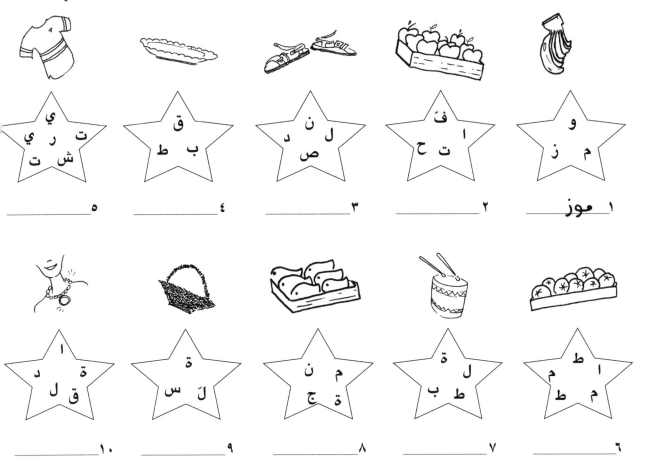

٦ ط ا م م ط — ____
٧ ة ل ب ط — ____
٨ م ن ة ج — ____
٩ ة لّ س — ____
١٠ ا ة د ق ل — ____

4 Make the words refer to two of something using the dual ending, as in the example.

١ سوق ← سوقان *(two markets)*　　٦ خاتم ← ____
٢ طَبَق ← ____　　٧ طَبلة ← ____
٣ سلّة ← ____　　٨ حقيبة ← ____
٤ كيس ← ____　　٩ قَلَم ← ____
٥ قَميص ← ____　　١٠ قِلادة ← ____

Tip: The dual ending has two alternatives: -ān (ان) and -ayn (يَن). Both endings are used in Modern Standard, depending on the context, but -ayn is more common in spoken dialects.

5 Rewrite this conversation in the bazaar in the right order, as in the example.

صندل جلد؟ الصندل الأبيَض جميل.

نعم، جميل. بكم هذا، من فضلك؟

لا، أريد صندل جِلد من فضلك.

نعم. عِندَنا هذا الصَندَل الجديد.

تفضّل. عشرة جنيهات.

أهلاً. صباح الخير!

صباح النور. هل عِندَكُم صَنادِل؟

شكراً، مع السلامة.

بعشرة جنيهات.

– أهلاً. صباح الخير!

6 How do you say these in Arabic?

١ How much is the drum? بكم الطبلة؟

٢ How much is a kilo of the apples? ______

٣ The necklace is ten pounds. ______

٤ The basket is seven pounds. ______

٥ A kilo of the tomatoes is three pounds. ______

٦ How much is the copper plate? ______

٧ The leather sandals are eight pounds. ______

7 **Conversation**

You are in the market and want to buy some fruit and vegetables from a stall.
Prepare your half of the conversation with the seller (البائع) and try saying it out loud.
Use the English prompts to guide you, as in the example.

أنت: *Do you have any oranges?* هل عندكم برتقال؟ hal ʿindakum burtuqāl?

البائع: عندنا إسبانيّ ومصريّ. ʿindanā isbānīy wa-miṣrīy.

أنت: *A kilo of the Egyptian oranges, please.* ______

البائع: تفضّل(ي). tafaḍḍal(ī).

أنت: *And how much are the potatoes?* ______

البائع: الكيلو بجنيه. al-kīlū bi-junayh.

أنت: *Three kilos, please. How much is that?* ______

البائع: ٩ جنيهات، من فضلك. tisʿa junayhāt, min faḍlak(-ik).

أنت: *Here you are. Do you have a bag?* ______

البائع: تفضّل(ي). مع السلامة. tafaḍḍal(ī). maʿa s-salāma.

unit 11

Plurals and colours

1 Identify the root letters of each word on the right and then fill in its meaning and plural.

Plural	Meaning	Root letters	Word
أقلام	pen	ق/ل/م	قَلَم
			طَبَق
			قَلب
			مُدَرِّس
			سِعر
			سيّارة
			سَيف
			وَلَد
			لَون
			حَفلة
			كوب
			شَمعة
			مُصَوِّر
			كيس
			مُمَرِّضة

2 Now describe what you own using the picture prompts, as in the example.

١  هذه هي أقلامي. (These are my pens.)

٢  ______

٣  ______

٤ 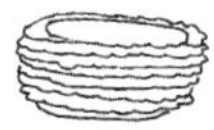 ______

٥  ______

٦ 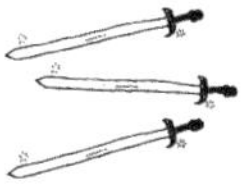 ______

٧  ______

٨  ______

٩  ______

١٠  ______

Tip: Only use the plural word هـؤلاء hā'ulā'i (these) and the pronouns هم hum/هنّ hunna (they) when referring to *people* in the plural. Remember that in Arabic the plural of objects is referred to in the *feminine singular*.

3 Use the key to colour the grid and reveal the picture.

٤	٤	٥	٤	٤	٤	٤	٤	٤	٤	٤
٤	٥	٥	٥	٥	٥	٥	٥	٥	٥	٤
٤	٦	٦	٦	٦	٦	٦	٦	٦	٦	٤
٤	٦	١	١	٦	٦	٦	١	١	٦	٤
٤	٦	١	١	٦	٦	٦	١	١	٦	٤
٤	٦	٦	٦	٦	٦	٦	٦	٦	٦	٤
٣	٦	٦	٦	٢	٢	٢	٦	٦	٦	٣
٣	٦	٦	٦	٢	٢	٢	٦	٦	٦	٣
٣	٦	٦	٦	٢	٢	٢	٦	٦	٦	٣

١ أبيض ٤ أزرق
٢ أسود ٥ أحمر
٣ أخضر ٦ أصفر

ما هذا؟

هذا ________ .

4 Ahmed is going on a trip to Paris and has made a list of all the things his family has asked him to bring back. Look at the list below and fill in the table on page 49 with the details of the items, as in the example.

بابا: قميص أبيض (قُطن) للحفلات
طارِق: حقيبة جلد سوداء للمدرسة
راندا: أقلام للكتابة (أحمر وأسود)
عادِل: خيمة زرقاء (خفيفة)
ماما: أفلام فرنسيّة قديمة
نونو: صندل بلاستيك صغير (أخضر)
ميمي: قبّعة صفراء (قطن أو حرير)

Who?	Item(s)	Description
Dad	shirt	white (cotton) for parties

5

Conversation

You are in a clothes shop and want to buy a cotton T-shirt and hat. Prepare your half of the conversation with the seller and try saying it out loud. Use the English prompts to guide you, as usual.

أنت: *I'd like a cotton T-shirt.* ______________________

البائع: حاضر. عندنا كلّ الألوان. ḥāḍir. ɛindanā kull il-alwān.

أنت: *I prefer the blue [one].* ______________________

البائع: تفضّل(ي). tafaḍḍal(ī).

أنت: *And do you have cotton hats?* ______________________

البائع: نعم... أيّ لون؟ naɛam... ayy lawn?

أنت: *The white hat.* ______________________

البائع: ٨ ريالات من فضلك. thamānyat riyālāt min faḍlak(-ik).

أنت: *Here you are. Thank you.* ______________________

unit 12

Eating and drinking

1 Find the food-related words in the word square. The words can read right to left or top to bottom. One is completed for you.

ل	ا	ق	ت	ر	ب	ث	ف	ز	ك	س	ع
ح	ن	ب	ي	ه	ة	م	ع	ط	م	ا	س
م	خ	س	م	ص	ي	ا	ن	و	ك	ظ	ي
ا	ر	ك	س	ا	ش	ض	ل	ز	ر	أ	ر
ة	ظ	و	م	ج	ا	ج	د	ج	و	ل	ح
ؤ	ل	ي	ص	ش	ي	ه	د	ة	ن	ب	ج
ن	ي	ت	ا	ي	ذ	ص	ر	غ	ة	ف	ع
ة	ز	ع	ط	س	ج	ك	م	س	ك	ي	ب
ز	و	م	ذ	خ	ر	و	د	م	و	ث	ي
ي	ة	ض	ي	ب	ي	ل	ح	غ	ا	ن	ض
ت	ز	ب	ق	ز	ك	ا	ن	ي	ط	ب	ك
ل	ا	ق	ب	ه	ذ	ح	ة	ر	ي	ص	ع

~~sugar~~	eggs
tea	juice
macaroni	grocer
rice	cola
cheese	milk
restaurant	bread
oranges	figs
biscuits	bananas
fish	oil
meat	chicken

2 Now choose a suitable container or measure for each food item, as in the example.

١ زُجاجة / كيس ... سكّر

٢ كيلو / لِتر ... فَواكِه

٣ زجاجة / قِطعة ... جبنة

٤ عُلبة / أنبوبة ... مكرونة

٥ لِتر / علبة   بيض

٦ نصف لِتر / قِطعة ... حليب

٧ زجاجة / أنبوبة ... زَيت

٨ نصف كيلو / لِتر ... عصير تفّاح

٩ رُبع لِتر / رُبع كيلو ... بُنّ

١٠ أنبوبة / كيس   مَعجون طماطم

Jamila is doing her weekly shop in the local grocery. Look at her shopping list and complete the conversation with the grocer, as in the example.

٣ عُلَب بسكويت
زجاجة عصير برتقال
نصف كيلو جبنة بيضاء
كيس سكّر
كيلو تفّاح أخضر
أنبوبة معجون أسنان
علبة مسحوق غسيل

البقّال: صباح الخير يا مدام.

جميلة: صباح النور. أعطِني من فضلك ثلاث عُلَب بسكويت و________ عصير.

البقّال: عصير تفاح؟

جميلة: لا، عصير ________ من فضلك. وأريد نصف كيلو ________ بيضاء.

البقّال: تفضّلي. شيء ثاني؟

جميلة: ________ سكّر وكيلو ________ أخضر.

البقّال: تحت أمرك.

جميلة: وهل عندكم معجون ________ و________ غسيل؟

البقّال: عندنا ________ غسيل يا مدام ولكن ليس عندنا معجون ________.

جميلة: طيِّب... علبة ________ غسيل من فضلك. كم الحساب؟

البقّال: خمسة وأربعين جنيهاً.

جميلة: تفضّل. مع السلامة.

Which item on her list did Jamila not manage to buy? And how much was the bill?

4 Yusuf has sent his sister Amina a message from Beirut to tell her about the Lebanese food he's been trying during his stay. Read the email and decide whether the sentences below are true or false. (*Note:* زَعتر zaɛtar = thyme.)

مساء الخير يا أمينة!

أنا الآن في مطعم لبناني صغير قريب من المدرسة مع أصحابي، وعلى المائدة هناك أطباق لبنانيّة كثيرة!

أنا أُحِب السلطات اللبنانيّة والخُبز وأحبّ اللحم والدجاج والكباب كذلك. ولكنّي لا أُحبّ الحلويات اللبنانيّة – فيها سكّر كثير جدّاً ! أُفضّل الفواكه: البرتقال والتفّاح والتين.

أنا طبقي اللبناني المفضّل اِسمه «المَناقيش»، وهو خُبز عربيّ مع الزَعتَر وزَيت الزَيتون. هذه هي صورة المَناقيش على مائدتنا... هَم! هَم!

مع حُبّي، أخوكِ يوسف

١ يوسف في مطعم كبير. ☐

٢ هو مع أصحابه. ☐

٣ المطعم في لبنان. ☐

٤ يُحِبّ يوسف السلطات اللبنانيّة والخبز. ☐

٥ لا يُحِبّ الدجاج أو اللحم. ☐

٦ الحلويات اللبنانيّة فيها حليب كثير جدّاً. ☐

٧ يفضّل يوسف الفواكه. ☐

٨ هذه صورة خبز عربيّ . ☐

٩ على الخبز هناك بيض وزَعتَر. ☐

١٠ هذا الطبق اِسمه «المَناقيش». ☐

Now imagine you are in a restaurant in a country you know. Decide where you are, who you are with, what local foods you like and don't like, and what your favourite dish is. Then, following Yusuf's model, fill in the gaps to create your own message to a family member.

مساء الخير يا ________ !

أنا الآن في مطعم ________ صغير قريب من ________ مع ________،
وعلى المائدة هناك أطباق ________ كثيرة!

أنا أُحِب ________ و________ وأحبّ ________ و________ كذلك.
ولكنّي لا أُحبّ ________ – فيها ________ كثير جدّاً ! أُفضّل
________: ________ و________.

هذه صورة ________ مع ________. أنا طبقي ________ المفضّل
هو «________»، وهذه هي صورة ________ على مائدتنا... هَم! هَم!

مع حُبّي، ________ ________

Conversation

You are in a restaurant ordering a meal. Follow the prompts to order from the waiter.

أنت: *Waiter! Please!* ________________

الجرسون: نعم! naɛam!

أنت: *I'll have grilled chicken with rice.* ________________

الجرسون: تحت أمرك. taḥt amrak(-ik)

أنت: *And I'd like the tomato salad.* ________________

الجرسون: والمشروب؟ wal-mashrūb?

أنت: *I'll have a cold orange juice.* ________________

الجرسون: هل تجرّب الحلويات بعد ذلك؟ hal tujarrib al-ḥalawīyyāt baɛda dhālik?

أنت: *Yes. The ice cream with fruit, please.* ________________

الجرسون: تحت أمرك. taḥt amrak(-ik)

unit 13

What happened yesterday?

1 Match the Arabic verbs to the English equivalents, as in the example.

I opened	**a**	شَرِبْتُ	١
I sat	**b**	خَرَجْتُ	٢
I heard	**c**	كَتَبْتُ	٣
I drank	**d**	فَتَحْتُ	٤
I found	**e**	رَجَعْتُ	٥
I went	**f**	أَكَلْتُ	٦
I returned	**g**	جَلَسْتُ	٧
I went out	**h**	سَمِعْتُ	٨
I ate	**i**	ذَهَبْتُ	٩
I wrote	**j**	وَجَدْتُ	١٠

2 Describe what you did yesterday, using the picture prompts and one of the verbs from Activity 1, as in the example.

١  شربتُ فنجان شاي.

٢  ______

٣  ______

٤  ______

٥  ______

٦  ______

٧  ______

٨  ______

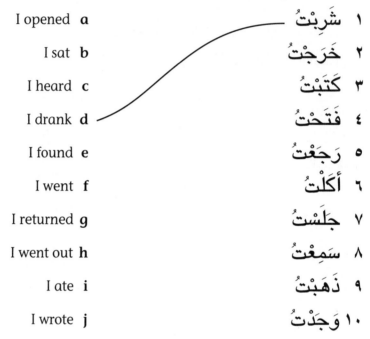

3 Write these verbs to refer to the correct person, as in the example.

١ ذهب (هي) ← ذَهَبَت (she went)

٢ شرب (أنا) ← ....

٣ كتب (هو) ← ....

٤ فتح (أنتَ) ← ....

٥ أكل (أنتِ) ← ....

٦ وجد (أنتَ) ← ....

٧ خرج (هو) ← ....

٨ جلس (أنتِ) ← ....

٩ سمع (هي) ← ....

١٠ فعل (أنا) ← ....

4 Read about the three people below and write notes in the table, as in the examples.

وَحيد يَعمَل في جريدة سوريّة. أمس صباحاً ذهب إلى مكتب الجريدة وكتب عن سَرِقة في بنك كبير. رجع إلى البيت مساءً وجلس مع زَوجته. أكل سمكاً وشرب قهوة.

ماري مُمرّضة . أمس ذهبَت إلى المستشفى صباحاً وبعد ذلك ذهبَت إلى السوق. رجعَت إلى البيت مساءً وكتبَت خِطاباً لأُختها. أكلَت سلطة بيض وشربَت فنجان شاي.

وَردة تِلميذة. أمس ذهبَت إلى المدرسة صباحاً وبعد ذلك ذهبَت إلى بيت صاحِبَتها. رجعَت مساءً وفَتَحَت زجاجة كولا وجلسَت أمام التليفزيون. أكلَت بيتزا مع البطاطس المحمّرة.

NAME	OCCUPATION	YESTERDAY			
		Did what daytime?	Did what evening?	Ate what?	Drank what?
Waheed	newspaper journalist	went to office wrote about theft			

5 Yusuf has written another email to his mother, this time about a trip he made yesterday to the town of Sidon (صيدا ṣaydā). Read the email and answer the questions in English.

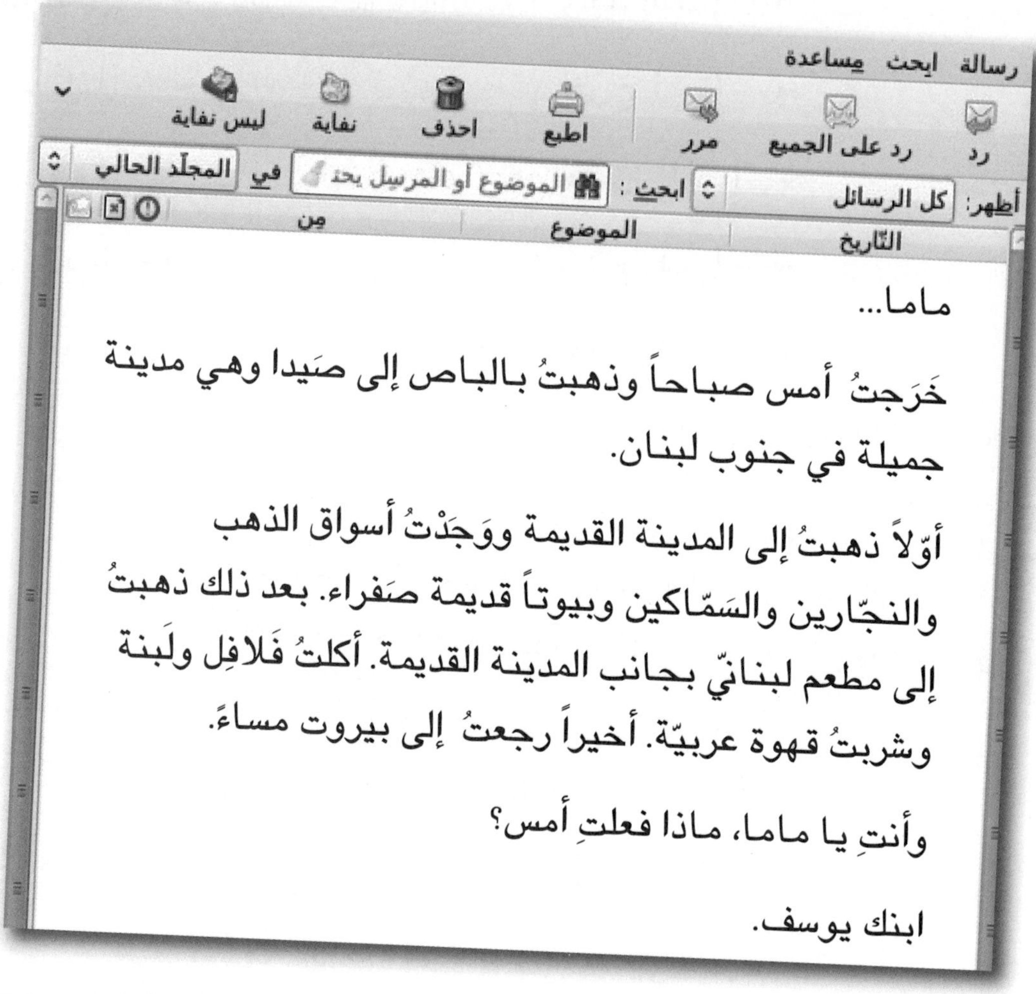

ماما...

خَرَجتُ أمس صباحاً وذهبتُ بالباص إلى صَيدا وهي مدينة جميلة في جنوب لبنان.

أوّلاً ذهبتُ إلى المدينة القديمة ووَجَدْتُ أسواق الذهب والنجّارين والسَمّاكين وبيوتاً قديمة صَفراء. بعد ذلك ذهبتُ إلى مطعم لبنانيّ بجانب المدينة القديمة. أكلتُ فَلافِل ولَبنة وشربتُ قهوة عربيّة. أخيراً رجعتُ إلى بيروت مساءً.

وأنتِ يا ماما، ماذا فعلتِ أمس؟

ابنك يوسف.

1 Where is Sidon?

2 How did Yusuf get there?

3 Where did he go first in Sidon?

4 How many markets did he find in the old city?

5 What type of markets were they?

6 What else did he see in the old city?

7 Where did he go after that?

8 What did he eat and drink?

9 When did he return to Beirut?

10 What question does he ask his mother at the end of the email?

6 Here is a description of what Yusuf did in Sidon. Without looking at the email on page 56, see whether you can fill in the gaps in the description, as in the example.

خَرَجَ يوسف أمس ___صباحاً___ وذَهَبَ بالباص __________ صَيدا،

وهي مدينة جميلة في __________ لبنان.

أوّلاً ذهب إلى __________ القديمة ووَجَد __________ الذهب

والخبّازين والسَمّاكين وبيوتاً قديمة صَفراء. بعد __________

ذهب إلى مطعم لبنانيّ و __________ فَلافِل ولَبنة و __________

قهوة عربيّة. __________ رجع إلى بيروت __________.

7 **Conversation**

An Arabic-speaking friend, Tamer, is asking you about what you did yesterday. Prepare your half of the conversation with him and try saying it out loud. Use the English prompts to guide you, as usual.

تامر: ماذا فعلت أمس؟ mādhā faɛalta(-ti) ams?

أنت: *I went to the gold market.* __________

تامر: وماذا وجدت؟ wa-mādhā wajadta(-ti)?

أنت: *I found a necklace for my sister.* __________

تامر: أين أكلت؟ ayna alkalta(-ti)?

أنت: *I ate in a Lebanese restaurant.* __________

تامر: جميل! وبعد ذلك؟ jamīl! wa-baɛda dhālik?

أنت: *I drank Arabic coffee.* __________

تامر: وهل خرجت مساءً؟ wa-hal kharajta(-ti) masā'an?

أنت: *No, I wrote email[s] to my friends.* __________

unit

14 Wish you were here

1 Identify the root letters of each word on the right, and then fill in its meaning and plural.

Plural	Meaning	Root letters	Word
كِلاب	dog	ك/ل/ب	كَلب
			رَجُل
			صورة
			جَبَل
			لُعبة
			غُرفة
			بَحر
			جَمَل
			عُلبة

2 Arrange these Arabic numbers from the smallest to the largest. The first is done for you.

a سبعة وأربعين
e مئة وثلاثين
j ستّة وستّين
b أحد عشر
f أربعة
i ثلاثة وعشرين
l واحد وخمسين
c ستّة عشر
g ثمانية وثلاثين
k خمسة عشر
m تسعة
d مئة وثلاثة
h اثنا عشر
n أربعين

f, ______________________________

3 أمس ذهبنا إلى السوق ... Yesterday we went to market ...

Describe what you found in a crowded market, as in the example.

٧  وجدنا سبعة جمال.

٤  ______

١٠  ______

٦  ______

٢٠  ______

١٤  ______

٣  ______

٣٣ 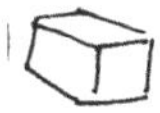 ______

١٥  ______

٥٠  ______

٨٦  ______

٩  ______

Tip: When writing Arabic numbers you will impress others if you can remember that:
- the plural is used only after numbers 3–10; 11 and upwards are followed by the *singular*
- the tā' marbūṭa (ة) is *removed* from numbers 3–10 when counting *feminine* nouns
- after numbers 11–99, the extra alif (اً) is added to the singular noun (unless ending in ة).

ثلاثة رجال (three men) ثلاثين رَجُلاً (thirty men)
ثلاث غُرَف (three rooms) ثلاثين غُرفة (thirty rooms)

4 Read the card from Iman to her sister Safa and choose the correct words to complete the sentences below, as in the example.

القَلعة القديمة، حمّامات، تونس

عزيزتي صفاء،

نحن في مدينة حمّامات في تونس والطقس مُشمِس وحارّ جدّاً. درجة الحرارة أربعون!
وجدنا فندقاً جميلاً في الشمال الشرقيّ بجانب البحر. وراء الفندق هناك شجر وجبال.

أمس ذهبنا أنا والأولاد إلى القَلعة القديمة ولكن آدَم كتب إيميل في الغُرفة. بعد ذلك أكلنا سمكاً بالكُسكُس في مطعم تونسيّ.

أخيراً ذهبتُ أنا إلى السوق ولكن آدَم والأولاد رجعوا إلى الفندق.

مع تحياتي، أختك إيمان

١ إيمان في...	مصر	(تونس)	فرنسا
٢ الطقس...	بارد	مُعتدل	حارّ
٣ درجة الحرارة...	٢٠	٣٠	٤٠
٤ الفندق بجانب...	البحر	المتحف	السوق
٥ أمس ذهبوا إلى...	القصر	القلعة	البحر
٦ في المطعم أكلوا...	دجاجة	سمكاً	بيتزا
٧ ذهبَت إيمان إلى...	السوق	البنك	المستشفى
٨ ولكن آدَم والأولاد رجعوا إلى...	القلعة	البيت	الفندق

Now find the Arabic equivalents of these expressions in the postcard, as in the example.

١ Dear Safa ________ عزيزتي صفاء

٢ sunny and very hot ________

٣ in the north-east ________

٤ trees and mountains ________

٥ the boys and I ________

٦ the old fort ________

٧ fish with couscous ________

٨ with my best wishes ________

Conversation

You are on holiday with your family in France and are talking to your friend, Tamer, over the internet.

أنت: *We're in the town of Avignon.* naḥnu fī madīnat afīnyūn.. نحن في مدينة أفينيون

تامر: كيف حال الطقس؟ kayfa ḥāl aṭ-ṭaqṣ?

أنت: *Rainy and cold. It's 15°.* ________

تامر: هل أنتم في فندق؟ hal antum fī funduq?

أنت: *No, we found a house in the old town.* ________

تامر: ماذا فعلتُم؟ mādhā faعaltum?

أنت: *Yesterday we went to the old palace ...* ________

and we sat beside the river. ________

تامر: جميل! jamīl!

أنت: *What did you do yesterday, Tamer?* ________

unit 15

Review

1 Count how many of each item there are in the toy-shop window, as in the example.

في الشبّاك هناك خمسة جمال، ثلاثة...

Complete the crossword in English using the Arabic clues. One clue is completed for you.

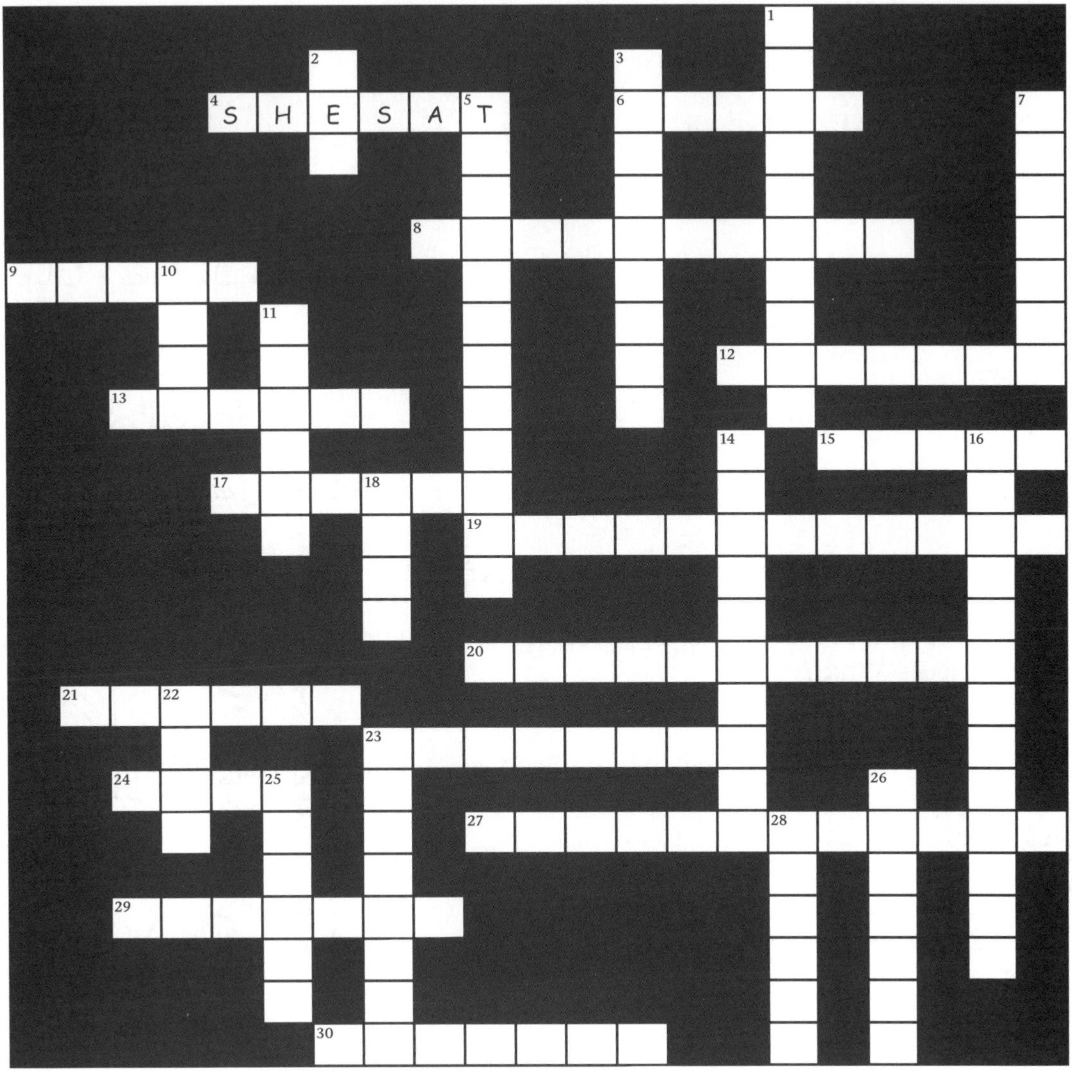

Across

4 جلَسَت (3,3)
6 ثمانية (5)
8 خاتم فضّة (6,4)
9 أسوَد (5)
12 زُجاجات (6)
13 شَرِبتُ (1,5)
15 جَنوب (5)
17 ذَهَبنا (2,4)
19 فِنجان قهوة (1,3,2,6)
20 تحت السرير (5,3,3)
21 سَمِعتُ (1,5)
23 أُختي (2,6)
24 تين (4)
27 رَجَعوا (4,8)
29 كَتَبَ (2,5)
30 إنجليزيّ (7)

Down

1 معرِض (10)
2 أحمَر (3)
3 أمس (9)
5 عاصِمَتهُم (5,7)
7 شُموع (7)
10 بارِد (4)
11 أطباق (6)
14 ثلاثة وخمسين (5-5)
16 الشَّرق الأوسَط (3,6,4)
18 بيض (4)
22 مَخرَج (4)
23 جَبَل (8)
25 سُيوف (6)
26 بُرتقال (7)
28 ثلاثين (6)

3 Match the questions to the answers, for example ١f.

١ ما عملك؟	a هناك ثلاثين.
٢ متى ذهبتَ إلى دِمشَق؟	b نعم. كتبتُه أمس.
٣ بكم كيلو البرتقال؟	c نحن من شمال لبنان.
٤ ماذا وَجَدَ ابنك في الشارع؟	d بخير، الحمد الله.
٥ أنتم من أين؟	e خاتم ذهب!
٦ كيف حالك؟	f أنا مهندس في مصنع كبير.
٧ هل كتبتِ الإيميل لأُختك؟	g ذهبتُ الأُسبوع الماضي.
٨ هناك كم ممرّضة في المستشفى؟	h بعشرة جنيهات.

Tip: Remember that ما mā is generally used in front of a noun and ماذا mādhā in front of a verb; both mean 'What?'

4 Imagine you are on holiday with your friends. Write a postcard to a relative based on the model and expressions on pages 60–1. Include the following information:

- in Moscow (موسكو)
- it's cloudy and very cold (zero degrees)
- found new hotel/north-west/next to exhibition centre (مَركَز المَعارِض)
- yesterday: visited large palace in centre of town/ate fried fish with potatoes and onions in Russian restaurant
- finally: went to museum/friends returned to hotel

How do you say these in Arabic?

1 I found the key under the chair. وجدتُ المفتاح تحت الكرسيّ.

2 The weather is very hot today. ______

3 We drank coffee in the market. ______

4 Did you *(pl.)* go to the museum? ______

5 They stayed in a small hotel. ______

6 I sat on the black chair near the door. ______

Conversation

Your friend Amira is taking you for a ride in her new car. You are asking her about a small bag she lost yesterday. Follow the prompts as usual to join in the conversation. (*Note*: seat = مقعد miqɛad)

أنت: *Did you find your bag?* ______

أميرة: لا. lā.

أنت: *Where did you go yesterday?* ______

أميرة: ذهبتُ إلى المطعم الجديد. dhahabtu ilā l-maṭɛam il-jadīd.

أنت: *Where did you sit in the restaurant?* ______

أميرة: بجانب الباب. bi-jānib al-bāb.

أنت: *And how did you return to the house?* ______

أميرة: بسيّارتي. bi-sayyāratī.

أنت: *Ahh ... Is your bag black?* ______

أميرة: نعم! هل وجدتُها؟ naɛam! hal wajadtahā?

أنت: *Yes, between my seat and the door!* ______

unit

16 Every day

1 كم الساعة؟. Write out the correct time, as in the example.

١  الساعة الثالثة

٢ 

٣ 

٤ 

٥ 

٦ 

٧ 

٨ 

٩ 

١٠ 

Sami is a mechanical engineer. Look at his work-day routine; then fill in the gaps in the paragraph using the information from the pictures, as in the example.

سامي مهندس ميكانيكيّ. كلّ يوم _يغسِل_ وَجهَهُ الساعة ________ ويَلبِس

مَلابِس العمل، ثُمّ ________ الإفطار الساعة السادسة و ________. عادةً يَخرُج

من البيت ________ السابعة ويَذهَب إلى مَصنَع السيّارات بالـ________. يَرجِع

من ________ إلى البيت الساعة ________ والرُّبع ويَرسُم صُوَراً للشَّجَر والجِبال

والأنهار بالألوان. يأكل ________ الساعة الثامنة إلا ________ وبعد ذلك يَشرَب

________ شاي. أخيراً ________ البيجاما ويَنام الساعة ________.

Note: **ملابس** malābis = clothes; **يرسم** yarsum = he draws

3 Amira is a pupil at school. Look at the prompts below and write notes in Arabic about her daily routine with times, as in the example.

تَصحو الساعة السادسة	wake up	
	put on school clothes	
	eat breakfast	
	leave house	
	go to school by bicycle	
	return from school	
	school work ('write lessons') play with little sister	
	eat dinner	
	drink glass of milk	
	put on pyjamas	
	sleep	

4 Imagine you are Amira. Write about your day, following the example on page 67.

أنا تلميذة في المدرسة. كلّ يوم أَصحو...

5 Change the verbs according to the pronoun in brackets, as in the example. Then choose from the verbs you have written to complete the five sentences below.

١ يَذهَب (هي) ← تَذهَب (she goes)	٥ يأكُل (أنتِ) ← ________
٢ يشرَب (أنا) ← ________	٦ يَلعَب (أنتَ) ← ________
٣ يَدرُس (هم) ← ________	٧ يَلبَس (أنتم) ← ________
٤ يَغسِل (نحن) ← ________	٨ يَكتُب (هم) ← ________

يا أولاد، هل ________ البيجامات؟

كلّ يوم أنا وأخي ________ الأطباق بعد العشاء.

بعد الغداء أجلس في كرسيّ و ________ فنجان قهوة.

هم ________ التاريخ من الساعة التاسعة حتّى الساعة العاشرة.

لماذا لا ________ كرة الريشة مع أُختك، يا أحمد؟

6 **Conversation**

You are talking to Ali about your everyday routine.

علي: ماذا تفعل(ين) كلّ اليوم؟ mādhā tafعal(-īna) kull yawm?

أنت: *We usually eat breakfast at 8 o'clock ...* ________

and I leave the house at 8:20. ________

علي: كيف تذهب(ين) إلى المكتب؟ kayfa tadh-hab(-īna) ilā l-maktab?

أنت: *I go to the centre of town by train ...* ________

then I go by bus to the office. ________

علي: وفي المساء؟ wa fīl-masā'?

أنت: *I return at 5:30 or 5:45 ...* ________

and we eat dinner at 7:30. ________

And you? What do you do every day? ________

unit 17

Comparing things

1 Identify the root letters of the adjective on the right and then fill in the comparative word with its meaning. (*Note*: سعيد saعīd = happy.)

Meaning	Comparative	Root letters	Adjective
bigger/larger	أَكـبَر	ك/ب/ر	كبير
			صغير
			جميل
			رخيص
			بارد
			قصير
			سَعيد
			سريع
			ثقيل
			جديد
			خفيف
			غَنيّ
			هامّ
			قَويّ
			حُلو

Tip: In the comparative, doubled (identical second and third) root letters are written together (خفيف khafīf/أخفّ akhaff, light/lighter), and final root letters و or ي are written as alif maqṣūra (غنيّ ghanī/أغنى aghnā, rich/richer).

2 Samira has a neighbour called Nadia who loves to boast! She always wants to go one better than Samira and have the biggest and best of everything in the street. You play the part of Nadia (ن) and respond to what Samira (س) says, as in the example.

س: بَيتي كبير. ن: بيتي أكبر من بيتك. هو أكبر بيت في الشارع!

س: اِبني طويل. ن: ....

س: بِنتي جميلة. ن: ....

س: خاتمي قديم. ن: ....

س: سيّارتي سريعة. ن: ....

س: درّاجتي جديدة. ن: ....

س: حقيبتي خفيفة. ن: ....

س: عصيري حُلو. ن: ....

س: زوجي غنيّ. ن: ....

س: قِلادتي غالية. ن: ....

3 Put the days of the week in order starting with *Saturday*, as in the example.

☐ يوم الثُلاثاء	☐ يوم الإثنَين	☐ يوم الجُمعة
☐ يوم الخَميس	☐ يوم الأَربِعاء	☐ يوم الأَحد
١ يوم السَّبت		

4 Look at the pictures of what Tariq usually does each week and fill in the table below.

ماذا فعل طارق؟	الصورة	يوم الأسبوع
يطبُخ السمك للعَشاء.	٢	الثلاثاء
يأكُل في مطعم إيرانيّ.		
يذهَب إلى البنك.		
يكتُب إيميل لاِبن أخته.		
يشرَب قهوة في بيت صاحبه.		
يلعَب مع الكلب خارج المدينة.		
يجلِس مع أمّه في بيتها.		

5 Imagine you are Tariq. Say what you usually do each week. Start with Sunday and write a sentence for each day of the week, as in the example.

يوم الأحد عادةً ألعَب مع الكلب خارِج المدينة.

Rewrite these sentences in the past, as in the example.

١ أنا في البنك. كُنتُ في البنك.

٢ هُم في المصنع. __________

٣ هي طبّاخة. __________

٤ هل أنتَ الأطوَل؟ __________

٥ هو مُمَثِّل. __________

٦ الغُرفة جميلة. __________

٧ نحن فُقَراء. __________

٨ هل أنتِ سعيدة؟ __________

٩ الأطباق جديدة. __________

١٠ هل أنتُم أصحاب؟ __________

Conversation

You are showing your friend Anwar some old photos of your grandfather (جدّ jadd) and grandmother (جدّة jadda).

أنت: *This is my grandfather.* __________

أنور: ماذا كان عمله؟ mādhā kāna ɛamaluh?

أنت: *40 years ago, he was an actor.* __________

أنور: في السينما؟ fī s-sīnimā?

أنت: *Yes, he was famous (شَهير).* __________

He was the richest man in the town! __________

أنور: وماذا عن جدّتك؟ wa-mādhā ɛan jaddatak(ik)?

أنت: *She was the best cook!* __________

Her desserts were delicious. __________

أنور: يا سلام! yā salām!

أنت: *I was the happiest child (طِفل) in the street!* __________

unit 18

Education and business

1 Match the Arabic school and university subjects to the English equivalents, for example **١e**.

a sport
b history
c Arabic
d engineering
e geography
f drawing/art
g law

h chemistry
i music
j English
k medicine
l mathematics
m science
n languages

١ الجُغرافيا
٢ الرِّياضة
٣ الموسيقى
٤ الطِبّ
٥ الإنجليزيّة
٦ العُلوم
٧ الرِّياضيّات

٨ الرَّسم
٩ اللُّغات
١٠ الكيمياء
١١ الحُقوق
١٢ العربيّة
١٣ التاريخ
١٤ الهَندَسة

2 Look at this school timetable and describe the pupils' day, as in the example.

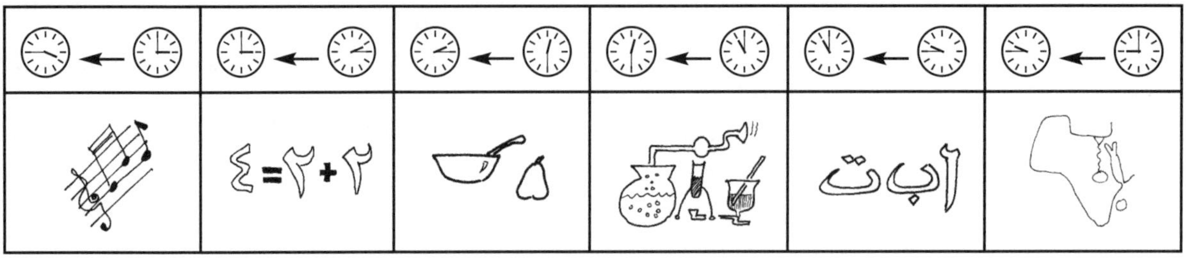

١ يدرُسون الجغرافيا من الساعة التاسعة حتّى العاشرة إلا رُبعاً.
٢
٣
٤
٥
٦

3 Complete this table of words with similar root patterns and give their meanings, as in the example.

Plural فعلاء	Person فعيل	Noun فعالة	Root letters
سُفَراء ambassadors	سَفير ambassador	سِفارة embassy	س/ف/ر
			و/ز/ر
			و/ك/ل
			ز/ع/م
			ر/ء/س
			ء/م/ر
			ز/م/ل

4 Put the Arabic business vocabulary into the word grid. The shaded squares will then spell out an additional item of vocabulary vertically. One is completed for you.

~~exhibition~~ meeting conference agency embassy council company

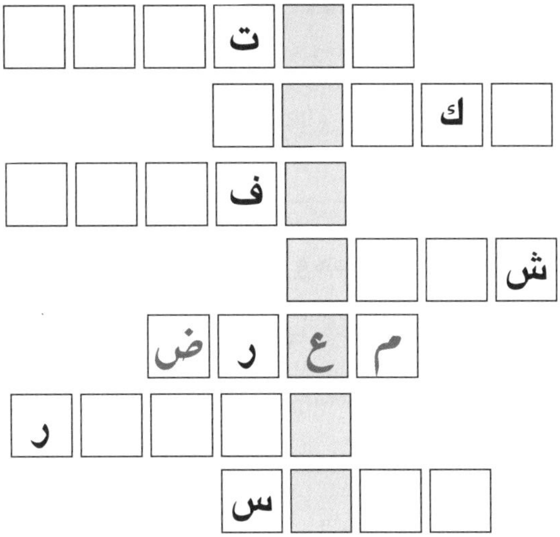

Additional vocabulary = ______________________ (meaning *workshop*, literally 'session of work')

5 Match the two halves of the sentences, for example ١d.

١ حضر السفير ...	a لِوزير التعليم.
٢ جلسَت وزيرة الصحّة مع ...	b الصناعة مُؤتَمَراً للمهندسين.
٣ كَتَبَت المدرّسة خطاباً ...	c الإمارات يوم الأحد.
٤ هل لعبتِ ...	d اِجتِماعاً مع الملك.
٥ أمس ذهبتُ ...	e «أنتُم لا تعرِفون الشَّعب.»
٦ بَدَأَت هذه ...	f عن السرقة في الفندق؟
٧ حضر وزير ...	g الممرّضات في المستشفى.
٨ هل سَمِعتَ ...	h إلى السفارة الفرنسيّة.
٩ قال رئيس الوزراء ...	i باللُعَب الجديدة في المعرض؟
١٠ رجعوا من ...	j الحَياة بعد اجتماع مَجلِس الوزراء.

6 Hashim works as a cleaner in the train station. His wife Zaynab, a nurse, and his son Tariq, an engineer, are discussing their work days tomorrow. They have all been told to make special arrangements. Complete the text using the words in the box, as in the example.

قال	يعمل	السادسة	هامّة	ابن
اسمها	المستشفى	الصفراء	~~هاشم~~	اليوم

هاشم عامِل نَظافة في مَحَطّة القطار. رئيس المحطّة قال له: ″يا (١) هاشم، اِغسِل القطار بالصابون (٢)____ لأن هناك راكِبة هامّة جدّاً على قطارنا هذا الصباح.″ زوجة هاشم ممرّضة (٣)____ زينب. قالَت زينب لزوجها هاشم: ″رئيس (٤)____ طلب من كلّ الأَطِبّاء والممرّضين والممرّضات أن يحضُروا اِجتِماعاً في مكتبه الساعة (٥)____ صباحاً لأن هناك زِيارة (٦)____ جدّاً للمستشفى صباح اليوم.″ طارق هو (٧)____ هاشم وزينب. (٨)____ طارق في مصنع أسمنت. (٩)____ طارق: ″صباح اليوم، طلب رَئيس الشركة مني ومن كلّ الزُملاء أن نُنَظِّف قبّعاتنا البلاستيكيّة (١٠)____، ولكن لا أعرِف لماذا!″

7 How do you say these in Arabic?

1 I returned from the Emirates on Friday. رجعتُ من الإمارات يوم الجمعة.

2 We study Arabic at ('in the') university. ______

3 Samira is the president of the company. ______

4 Every Wednesday she attends a meeting with the advertising agency. ______

5 I don't like mathematics or science. ______

6 I prefer history and languages. ______

8 **Conversation**

You are talking to your friend, Abdullah, about a conference you attended last Thursday.

عبد الله: ماذا فعلت الخميس الماضي؟ mādhā faʿalta(-ti) al-khamīs al-māḍī?

أنت: *I went to the Ministry of Industry.* ______

عبد الله: لماذا؟ li-mādhā?

أنت: *I attended a large conference ...* ______

عبد الله: مع من؟ maʿa man?

أنت: *with engineers from the Middle East.* ______

عبد الله: ما شاء الله! mā shā' allāh!

أنت: *The Prime Minister attended.* ______

عبد الله: رئيس الوزراء؟ ra'īs al-wuzarā'?

أنت: *Yes, and I sat next to him.* ______

unit

19 Future plans

1 Put the months of the year in order starting with *January*, as in the example.

☐ أبريل	☐ فَبراير	☐ ديسمبر
☐ أغُسطُس	☐ يونيو	☐ مايو
١ يَنايِر	☐ نوفمبِر	☐ مارِس
☐ أكُتوبِر	☐ يوليو	☐ سَبتَمبِر

2 Now write the day and date shown on the calendar, as in the example.

١ يوم الخميس، ١٥ يناير

٢ ______________

٣ ______________

٤ ______________

٥ ______________

٦ ______________

٧ ______________

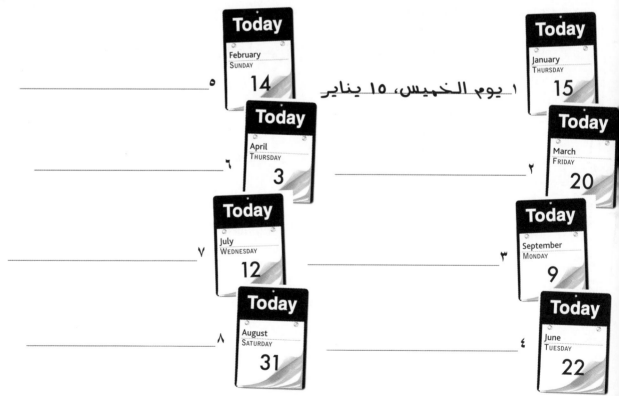

٨ ______________

A tour guide is telling her group what they will be doing the next day in Luxor (الأقصر al-aqṣur). Read what she says and complete the itinerary. (*Note:* معبد maعbad = temple; وادي wādī = valley.)

غداً سَتَزورون الأَقصر. الإفطار الساعة الخامسة والثُلث
صباحاً وسنأخذ الباص الساعة السادسة إلى وادي المُلوك غَرب النهر.
بعد ثلاث ساعات في وادي الملوك سنذهب إلى المتحف الفِرعونيّ في وسط المدينة.
الغداء في مطعم «آمون» بجانب مَعبَد الكَرنَك المشهور، وبعد الغداء
سَتَزورون المعبد. سنرجع إلى الفندق للعشاء الساعة الثامنة.

Wonders of the Nile عجائب النيل

Day 6: Luxor يوم ٦: الأقصر

Breakfast at __________ AM

Leave hotel at __________ AM

Visits:

1 ______________________________

2 ______________________________

(*Lunch:* __________ *Restaurant*)

3 ______________________________

Return to hotel at __________ PM

4 Basma has a busy day tomorrow. She has written down everything she needs to do so that she doesn't forget. Make sentences about her plans, as in the example.

١ سَتَزور أمّها في المستشفى الساعة التاسعة والنصف.

٢ ....

٣ ....

٤ ....

٥ ....

٦ ....

٧ ....

٩:٣٠ أمّي في المستشفى

١١:٢٠ اجتماع في المدرسة

١٣:٠٠ غداء مع مُنيرة

١٤:١٥ إلى البقّال

١٦:٠٠ إيميل للبنك

١٧:٠٠ غسل الملابس

١٨:٣٠ طبخ اللحم للعشاء

5 Choose one of the future verbs in the box to complete each sentence, as in the example.

سَتأكُل سَيدرُس سَأرجِع سَأُسافِر ~~سَيَحضُر~~

سَيزورون سَتَطيرين سَنُقابِل سَيذهَب

١ غدا سَيَحضُر الوزير اِجتماعاً في القصر الملكيّ.

٢ بعد غَد .... إلى بيتي مع زوجتي.

٣ .... نَبيل التاريخ الفرنسيّ في جامعة باريس.

٤ .... رئيس الشركة الساعة السادسة والنصف صباحاً.

٥ هل .... في المطعم الجديد يا أحمد؟

٦ بعد الاِمتِحانات .... إلى قَطَر. آمَل أن أعمَل كَممرّضة هناك.

٧ .... الأولاد إلى القاهرة و.......... المتحف المصريّ.

٨ متى .... إلى عُمان، يا سميرة؟

You are going on an extended study and leisure visit to Jordan. Write a note to a friend telling him or her about your plans. Include the following information:

- January 3: Fly to Jordan (at 4 AM!)
- January and February: Study Arabic in Amman University.
- March: Hope to travel by bus to Aqaba (العَقَبة).
- Stay in small hotel by the Red Sea. Would like to visit Petra (البَتراء).
- April: Finally return home.

Conversation

You are on holiday in Egypt. Your Egyptian friend, Adam, is asking you about your plans for the next couple of days.

آدم: ماذا ستفعلون غداً وبعد غد؟ mādhā sa-tafعalūna ghadan wa-baعda ghad?

أنت: *Tomorrow we'll go to Luxor by train.* ____________

آدم: هل الرحلة طويلة؟ hal ar-riḥla ṭawīla?

أنت: *Yes, we'll travel for 9 hours.* ____________

آدم: أين ستنامون؟ ayna sa-tanāmūna?

أنت: *We'll sleep on ['in'] the train.* ____________

آدم: وماذا ستفعلون في الأقصر؟ wa-mādhā sa-tafعalūna fīl-aqṣur?

أنت: *On Saturday we'll visit the Valley of the Kings.* ____________

أنت: *And we'll go to Karnak Temple on Sunday.* ____________

آدم: جميل! رحلة سعيدة! jamīl! riḥla saعīda!

unit 20 Review

1 Replace the underlined time phrase with the one in brackets. Change the tense of the verb to match the new time phrase, as in the example.

١ كلّ يوم يَرجِعون الساعة الرابعة. (أمس) أمس رجعوا الساعة الرابعة.

٢ في الماضي درستُ العربيّة (في المستقبل) ______

٣ الآن هو رَجُل فقير. (منذُ عشرين سنة) ______

٤ بَدَأنا الدِراسة مُنذُ شهرَين. (بَعدَ شهرَين) ______

٥ هل ستجلِس مع جَدّك غداً؟ (أمس) ______

٦ أين قابَلتِ زينة الخميس الماضي؟ (غداً) ______

٧ أوّل أمس سافرَت الوزيرة بالقطار. (عادةً) ______

٨ بعد أسبوع سيحضُر مُؤتَمَراً. (مُنذُ أسبوع) ______

2 Make these sentences negative, using لا lā, لم lam or ليس laysa, as in the example.

١ عندنا عُنوان الشركة. ليس عندنا عُنوان الشركة.

٢ أشرب الشاي في المساء. ______

٣ ذهبَتْ فاطمة إلى مكتبها. ______

٤ لي بيت قديم في الريف. ______

٥ هناك مفتاح لِهذا الباب. ______

٦ نسمع السيّارات من الشبّاك. ______

٧ جَرَّبنا الكمبيوتر الجديد في المعرض. ______

٨ لماذا سافَرتُم أمس صباحاً؟ ______

Complete the crossword in English, using the Arabic clues. One clue is completed for you.

Across

4 نغسل (2,4)

6 الأكبر في العالم (3,7,2,3,5)

7 طَبَخَت الغداء (3,6,5)

10 رياضة (5)

12 شهر (5)

14 بالقطار (2,5)

15 مِن (4)

17 أغنى من الملك (6,4,3,4)

19 متى؟ (4)

23 يلعبون (4,4)

24 موسيقى (5)

25 أدرس (1,5)

26 روسيا (6)

Down

1 أيّ؟ (5)

2 هامّ (9)

3 (الساعة) الرابعة والنصف (4,4,4)

5 قطعة جبنة (1,5,2,6)

8 عادةً (7)

9 مطاعم (11)

11 كلّ يوم (6,3)

13 غداً (8)

15 مستقبل (6)

16 محاضرة (7)

18 معجون أسنان (10)

20 نوفمبر (8)

21 لحم (4)

22 مسجد (6)

23 اليوم (5)

4 Read the magazine profile of a prominent businessman, Mohammed Abbas, and answer the questions. There may be one or two unfamiliar words, but try to get the gist.

Tip: Remember to start with the *right-hand* column.

1 What were Mohammed's father's profession and working hours?
2 How many rooms did the family house have?
3 On which days did he help his father?
4 Was Mohammed's family well off when he was a boy? What about now?
5 How many bakeries does he own and where are they?
6 Where does he live now and with whom?
7 Was Mohammed happy as a boy? How does he describe his parents?
8 What does he still do today in the morning that he did as a boy?

مُنذُ ثلاثين سنة كان محمّد عبّاس ولداً فقيراً. أبوه، الشيخ عبّاس، كان خبّازاً صغيراً يَعمَل في مَخبَزه كلّ يوم من الساعة الرابعة صباحاً حتّى الساعة السابعة مساءً. كان لَهُم بَيت صغير من غُرفَتَين: غُرفة للوالدَين وغُرفة للأولاد السبعة.

كان محمد أكبر ولد، ولذلك كان يعمل مع والده في المخبز أيام الخميس والجمعة والسبت.

هذا الولد الفقير هو الآن رَجُل لَهُ أكثر من تسعين مخبزاً في الشرق الأوسط. بيته قَصر جميل وكبير بجانب النهر، يَعيش فيه مع زوجته وأولاده.

يَقول محمد عبّاس «نعم، أنا كُنتُ فقيراً، ولكنّي كنتُ سَعيداً. أبي كان رَجُلاً قَويّاً وعرفتُ مِنه حُبّ العمل. وأمّي كانَت كريمة وجميلة وكانت أفضل طبّاخة في الشارع! كُنّا فُقَراء، ولكن كنّا نأكل خُبزاً دافِئاً مع قِطعة جُبنة كلّ صباح.»

محمّد عبّاس هو اليوم أهمّ وأغنى رجل في المدينة، له أشهَر مَخابِز في العالَم العربيّ وإلى اليوم يأكل كلّ صباح خبزاً دافئاً وقِطعة جُبنة لِلإفطار مع أولاده.

5 Find the Arabic in the article for the words and expressions below, as in the example.

١ bakery/bakeries مَخبَز / مَخابِز
٢ for the (two) parents ____________
٣ and for that (reason) ____________
٤ his parent (father) ____________
٥ he lives ____________
٦ I was happy ____________
٧ the love of work ____________
٨ warm bread ____________
٩ most famous ____________
١٠ until today ____________

6 How do you say these in Arabic?

1 Jamila plays badminton in the club. تَلعَب جميلة كُرة الريشة في النادي.

2 I usually wake up at half-past seven. ____________

3 We eat fruit every day. ____________

4 The Nile is the longest river in the world. ____________

5 I'll write you *(masc.)* an email tomorrow. ____________

6 How will they travel to Luxor? ____________

7 **Conversation**

You are back from Luxor now and you are telling your Egyptian friend, Adam, about the rest of your stay in Cairo, including a visit to the university and mosque of Al-Azhar (الأزهر).

آدم: متى رجعتُم من الأقصر؟ matā rajaعtum min al-aqṣur?

أنت: *We returned from Luxor on Monday.* ____________

And yesterday we visited Al-Azhar. ____________

It's the oldest university in the world. ____________

آدم: نعم، والمسجد جميل. naعam, wal-masjid jamīl.

أنت: *After that, we ate pigeon with Arabic bread. It was delicious!*

____

آدم: ومتى سترجعون؟ wa-matā sa-tarjiعūn?

أنت: *We will fly tomorrow at 3 AM.* ____________

آدم: الساعة الثالثة؟! as-sāعa ath-thālitha?!

أنت: *So I'll say 'goodbye' now.* ____________

But I'll study Arabic every day. ____________

I know the best book in the world! ____________

Answers to activities

unit 1 Getting started

Activity 1
3 bu, 7 tha, 6 yu, 10 ya, 1 ba, 9 tu, 4 thi, 8 ni, 2 ti, 5 na

Activity 2
1 نُ
2 تَ
3 بِ
4 ثُ
5 يِ
6 ثَ
7 بُ
8 تُ

Activity 3

At the end	In the middle	At the beginning	Letter
ـب	ـبـ	بـ	(bā') ب
ـت	ـتـ	تـ	(tā') ت
ـث	ـثـ	ثـ	(thā') ث
ـن	ـنـ	نـ	(nūn) ن
ـي	ـيـ	يـ	(yā') ي

Activity 4
ثابت البنا وزير التعليم اللبناني
في البيت الأبيض يوم الثلاثاء

ي 7 ن 3 ث 3 ت 3 ب 5

Activity 5
Handwriting practice. *Try to show your handwriting to an Arabic-speaking teacher or friend.*

Activity 6
1b, 2a, 3b, 4c, 5c, 6c, 7a, 8b

Activity 7
1 بَيت
2 تِبن
3 بَين
4 بُنّ
5 بِنت

Activity 8
1 صباح النور ṣabāḥ an-nūr
2 مساء النور masā' an-nūr
3 أهلاً بكَ ahlan bik(a)
4 أهلاً بكِ ahlan biki

unit 2 Putting words together

Activity 1

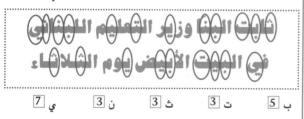

Activity 2
1 نور
2 زين
3 أندي
4 باري
5 زيد
6 أنور
7 داني
8 نادر
9 دينا
10 ثابت

Activity 3
1 دينا وَنور 2 أندي وَزين 3 أنور وَزيد
4 ثابت وَباري 5 نور وَداني 6 باري وَنادر
7 أنور وَدينا 8 نادر وَأندي

Activity 4
Handwriting practice. *Try to show your handwriting to an Arabic-speaking teacher or friend.*

Activity 5
1b, 2a, 3b, 4c, 5a, 6c

Activity 6

1 أنا زيد.
2 أنا نور وأنتِ؟
3 أنا بدر وأنتَ؟
4 أنا داني.
5 أنتَ أنور؟
6 أنتِ زينب؟

Activity 7

أنت: أهلاً يا زينب. ahlan yā zaynab.
زينب: أهلاً بك. ahlan bik(a)/biki.
أنت: كيف الحال؟ kayf al-ḥāl?
زينب: الحمد الله. al-ḥamdu lillāh.
أنت: أنت أنور؟ anta anwar?
أنور: نعم، أنا اسمي أنور. naعam, anā ismī anwar.
أنت: تشرّفنا يا أنور. tasharrafnā yā anwar.
أنور: تشرّفنا. tasharrafnā.

unit 3 The family

Activity 1

1d, 2a, 3f, 4c, 5b, 6e

Activity 2

Handwriting practice. *Try to show your handwriting to an Arabic-speaking teacher or friend.*

Activity 3

ث	ا	ذ	د	ت	ي	ب
ة	ر	خ	م	ر	ه	ن
ج	ب	ي	ت	ي	ذ	ت
ر	ا	م	ح	ذ	ث	ر
ي	ث	ة	ج	ا	ج	د
د	ا	م	ح	ب	م	ه
ة	ج	ا	ج	ز	ي	ذ

1 زُجاجة F
2 بَيت M
3 جَريدة F
4 حِمار M
5 بِنت F
6 خَيمة F
7 دَجاجة F
8 نَهر M

Activity 4

1 أخي
2 أبي
3 أمّي
4 أختي
5 ابني
6 بنتي
7 زوجي
8 زوجتي
9 بيتي
10 مدينتي

Activity 5

1 مها
2 أيمن
3 ماري
4 حامد
5 بدر
6 زيزي

Activity 6

1 هذا زوجي، حامد.
2 هذه أمّي، مها.
3 ماري هي بنت أيمن.
4 نادية هي زوجة حامد.
5 مَن (هو) بدر؟ هو ابني.
6 من (هي) ماري؟ هي بنتي.

Activity 7

زينب: أهلاً. ahlan.
أنت: كيف الحال يا زينب؟ kayf al-ḥāl yā zaynab?
زينب: الحمد لله. al-ḥamdu lillāh.
أنت: زينب، هذا أبي. zaynab, hādhā abī.
زينب: تشرّفنا. ومن هذه؟ tasharrafnā. wa-man hādhihi?
أنت: هذه أختي، ميمي. hādhihi ukhtī, mīmī.
زينب: أهلاً يا ميمي! ahlan yā mīmī!
أنت: آه... هذا هو قطاري. āh... hādhā huwa qiṭārī.
زينب: مع السلامة! maعa s-salāma!
أنت: مع السلامة! maعa s-salāma!

unit 4 Jobs

Activity 1

At the end	In the middle	At the beginning	Letter
ـس	ـسـ	سـ	(sīn) س
ـش	ـشـ	شـ	(shīn) ش
ـص	ـصـ	صـ	(ṣād) ص
ـض	ـضـ	ضـ	(ḍād) ض

Activity 2

Handwriting practice. *Try to show your handwriting to an Arabic-speaking teacher or friend.*

Activity 3

زيدان	7	أمين	2
ميدو	9	منير	1
حبيب	10	خيري	4
شحاتة	8	حمدي	3
نصري	11	أبو زيد	5
حسن	6		

Activity 4

Name	Relationship to Sara	Job
Sara	——	teacher
Hassan	husband	photographer
Yasmin	daughter	accountant
Amin	son	engineer
Samira	mother	nurse

Activity 5

1 هم نجّارون. 2 هم خبّازون.
3 نحن مهندسون. 4 هنّ مدرّسات.
5 نحن محاسبات. 6 هم مصوّرون.
7 هنّ مهندسات. 8 هنّ ممرّضات.

Activity 6

أنت: ما عملك يا سارة؟ mā ɛamalik yā sāra?

سارة: أنا مدرّسة. وأنت؟ anā mudarrisa. w-anta(-i)?

أنت: أنا طالب(ة). أبي خبّاز. anā ṭālib(a). abī khabbāz.

سارة: آه! أنا أخي خبّاز! āh! anā akhī khabbāz!

أنت: ما عمل زوجك؟ mā ɛamal zawjik?

سارة: هو مصوّر. huwa muṣawwir.

أنت: وابنك وبنتك؟ wa-ibnik wa-bintik?

سارة: أمين مهندس وياسمين محاسبة.
amīn muhandis wa-yāsmīn muḥāsiba.

أنت: ما شاء الله! mā shā' allāh!

unit 5 Describing things

Activity 1

1c, 2a, 3e, 4d, 5f, 6b

Activity 2

Handwriting practice. *Try to show your handwriting to an Arabic-speaking teacher or friend.*

Activity 3

1 قَلَم 2 دَرّاجة 3 كِتاب 4 خَيمة
5 قَميص 6 سَيّارة 7 خاتِم 8 مِفتاح
9 كَلب 10 حَقيبة

Activity 4

هذا...	هذه...
هذا قلم.	هذه درّاجة.
هذا كتاب.	هذه خيمة.
هذا قميص.	هذه سيّارة.
هذا خاتم.	هذه حقيبة.
هذا مفتاح.	
هذا كلب.	

Activity 5

1 ✔ 2 ✘ 3 ✔ 4 ✔ 5 ✘ 6 ✔ 7 ✘ 8 ✔

Activity 6

1 البيت 2 الولد 3 النهر 4 الزجاجة
5 المفتاح 6 الجريدة 7 التلميذ 8 القلم
9 المدينة 10 الخبّاز

Activity 7

أنت: صباح الخير. ṣabāḥ al-khayr

البائع: صباح النور. ṣabāḥ an-nūr

أنت: ممكن قلم من فضلك؟ mumkin qalam min faḍlak.

البائع: هذا القلم؟ hādhā l-qalam?

أنت: لا، أريد الأسود. lā, urīd al-aswad.

البائع: تَفَضَّل(ي). tafaḍḍal(ī).

أنت: هذا القلم مكسور! hādhā l-qalam maksūr!

البائع: آه! تَفَضَّل(ي). هذا القلم سليم.
ah! tafaḍḍal(ī). hādhā l-qalam salīm.

أنت: شكراً. shukran.

البائع: مع السلامة. maɛa s-salāma.

أنت: مع السلامة. maɛa s-salāma.

unit 6 Where is it?

Activity 1

At the end	In the middle	At the beginning	Letter
ـط	ـطـ	طـ	ط (ṭā')
ـظ	ـظـ	ظـ	ظ (ẓā')
ـع	ـعـ	عـ	ع (ɛayn)
ـغ	ـغـ	غـ	غ (ghayn)

Activity 2

1 عرب 2 طالب 3 عمل 4 غزّة

5 طنجة 6 بغداد 7 صنعاء 8 أبوظبي

Activity 3

1e, 2f, 3a, 4c, 5b, 6d

Activity 4

Handwriting practice. *Try to show your handwriting to an Arabic-speaking teacher or friend.*

Activity 5

Your answers may vary slightly.

1 الخاتم تحت الكرسيّ. 2 المفتاح في الباب.

3 الشبّاك فوق السرير. 4 هل الكتاب في السيّارة؟

5 هل الحقيبة على الخزانة؟ 6 الصورة بجانب التليفزيون.

7 السرير بين الشبّاك والمائدة.

8 هل الدراجة بين السيّارة والخيمة؟

Activity 6

Free writing. *Try to show your sentences to an Arabic-speaking teacher or friend.*

Activity 7

1 هل هذا سرير؟ 2 هل هذا شبّاك؟

3 هل هذه صورة؟ 4 هل هذا باب؟

5 هل هذا تليفزيون؟ 6 هل هذه خزانة؟

7 هل هذا مركب؟ 8 هل هذه مائدة؟

Activity 8

أنت: مساء الخير. masā' al-khayr

المتر: مساء النور. أهلاً وسهلاً.
masā' an-nūr. ahlan wa-sahlan.

أنت: أريد مائدة من فضلك. urīd mā'ida min faḍlak.

المتر: نعم. تَفَضَّل(ي). هذه المائدة؟
naʿam. tafaḍḍal(ī). hādhihi l-mā'ida?

أنت: لا. أريد مائدة بجانب الشبّاك من فضلك.
lā. urīd mā'ida bi-jānib ash-shabbāk, min faḍlak.

المتر: نعم. هذه المائدة؟ naʿam. hādhihi l-mā'ida?

أنت: نعم! المائدة تحت الصورة.
naʿam! al-mā'ida taḥt aṣ-ṣūra.

المتر: نعم. تَفَضَّل(ي). naʿam. tafaḍḍal(ī).

أنت: جميل! شكراً! jamīl! shukran!

unit 7 Describing places

Activity 1

Handwriting practice. *Try to show your handwriting to an Arabic-speaking teacher or friend.*

Activity 2

1 مصنع صغير 2 المصنع الصغير

3 مدينة كبيرة 4 المدينة الكبيرة

5 قميصي الجديد 6 كلبه الأسود الكبير

7 هو قويّ 8 هي بنت طويلة

Activity 3

1 Beirut (بيروت). 2 Yes. 3 Big. 4 Yes. 5 No. 6 In the centre of town. 7 An old, beautiful house. 8 An ugly factory and a large hospital. 9 The large hospital. 10 'Your son, Yusuf'.

Activity 4

✗1 ✗2 ✔3 ✔4 ✗5 ✗6 ✗7 ✔8

✔9 ✔10 ✗11 ✗12 ✔13 ✔14 ✔15 ✗16

✔17 ✗18

Activity 5

في هذه الصورة هناك شجرة كبيرة. أمام الشجرة هناك مائدة ثقيلة وكرسيّ. بجانب الكرسيّ هناك دجاجة صغيرة.

في وسط الصورة هناك ولد وهو على المائدة.
بجانب الولد هناك بنت. كلب البنت أسود وأبيض.

على المائدة هناك زجاجة كولا ووردة ولكن ليس هناك قلم أو كتاب.

Activity 6

أنت: صباح الخير. ṣabāḥ al-khayr

الرجل: صباح النور. ṣabāḥ an-nūr

أنت: البنك من أين من فضلك؟ al-bank min ayna min faḍlak?

الرجل: خد ثاني شارع على اليسار.
khud thāni shāriʿ ʿalā l-yasār.

أنت: هل البنك قريب من المدرسة؟
hal al-bank qarīb min al-madrasa?

الرجل: نعم. بجانب المدرسة. naʿam. bijānib al-madrasa.

أنت: شكراً. مع السلامة. shukran. maʿa s-salāma.

الرجل: مع السلامة. maʿa s-salāma.

unit 8 Review

Activity 1

Sun/moon letter	Arabic script	Name of letter
sun	ض	ḍād
sun	ط	ṭā'
sun	ظ	ẓā'
moon	ع	ɛayn
moon	غ	ghayn
moon	ف	fā'
moon	ق	qāf
moon	ك	kāf
sun	ل	lām
moon	م	mīm
sun	ن	nūn
moon	ه	hā'
moon	و	wāw
moon	ي	yā'

Sun/moon letter	Arabic script	Name of letter
moon	ا	alif
moon	ب	bā'
sun	ت	tā'
sun	ث	thā'
moon	ج	jīm
moon	ح	ḥā'
moon	خ	khā'
sun	د	dāl
sun	ذ	dhāl
sun	ر	rā'
sun	ز	zāy
sun	س	sīn
sun	ش	shīn
sun	ص	ṣād

Activity 2

Activity 3

1 بيتها 2 أبي 3 كتابه 4 غرفتي

5 ابنكَ 6 درّاجتكِ 7 زوجها 8 مدرستنا

9 مدينتهم 10 سيّارتهم

Activity 4

1F, 2F, 3T, 4T, 5F, 6T, 7F, 8T, 9T, 10F

Activity 5

1 الجريدة تحت الكرسيّ. 2 هناك كلب في الغرفة.

3 ليس هناك مدرسة في هذه المدينة. 4 هل بيتكَ كبير؟

5 هذه هي حقيبة زين. 6 أين أمّي؟ هي في البنك.

Activity 6

Note: From Unit 8 onwards, the answers to the end-of-unit conversations include only the missing lines which you say.

أنت: اسمي توم لويس. ismī Tom Lewis.

أنت: شكراً. أين غرفتي؟ shukran. ayna ghurfatī?

أنت: حقيبتي في السيّارة. الحقيبة ثقيلة!
ḥaqībatī fīs-sayyāra. al-ḥaqība thaqīla!

أنت: وهل هناك إنترنت في الغرفة؟
wa-hal hunāka internet fīl-ghurfa?

أنت: شكراً. shukran.

unit 9 Countries and people

Activity 1

1d, 2e, 3i, 4j, 5h, 6a, 7f, 8c, 9g, 10b

Activity 2

1 عمّان في شمال الأردن. 2 طرابلس في غرب ليبيا.

3 نيو يورك في شرق أمريكا. 4 لندن في جنوب إنجلترا.

5 بيروت في غرب لبنان. 6 *your [nearest] city*

Activity 3

Name	Nationality	Home town
Tom	English	Oxford
Natalia	Russian	Moscow
Maria	American	Los Angeles
Amna	Libyan	Tripoli
Ahmed	Saudi	Jeddah

Activity 4

1 هو فرنسيّ. 2 هو عراقيّ. 3 هي سوريّة.

4 هو إيطاليّ. 5 هي سودانيّة. 6 هم مصريّون.

7 هم إنجليز. 8 هنّ يابانيّات.

Activity 5

جاك فرنسيّ من باريس. أبو جاك من تولوز في جنوب فرنسا ولكن أُمّه من بيروت في لبنان. جاك محاسب في البنك اللبنانيّ في وسط المدينة. أبو جاك مهندس في مصنع صغير وأُخته مصوّرة في جريدة لُبنانيّة. أمّ جاك ممرّضة في مستشفى بجانب بَيتهم.

Activity 6

Free writing. *Try to show your description to an Arabic-speaking teacher or friend.*

Activity 7

أنت: أنت من أين يا سارة؟ anti min ayna yā sāra?

أنت: أنا إنجليزي(ة)... anā ingilīzīyya...

ولكن أمّي أمريكيّة. wa-lākinn ummī amrīkīyya.

أنت: أنا من ليدز. anā min Leeds.

أنت: هي في شمال إنجلترا. hiya fī shamāl ingiltarā.

أنت: لا، هي مدينة كبيرة. la, hiya madīna kabīra.

unit 10 Counting things

Activity 1

٦a, ٣b, ١c, ٧d, ٤e, ١٠f, ٢g, ٩h, ٨i, ٥j

Order: c, g, b, e, j, a, d, i, h, f

Activity 2

١ أربعة جنيهات ٢ ستّة جنيهات ٣ ثلاثة جنيهات

٤ عشرة جنيهات ٥ سبعة جنيهات ٦ جنيه واحد

٧ ثمانية جنيهات ٨ تسعة جنيهات

Activity 3

١ موز ٢ تفّاح ٣ صندل ٤ طبق ٥ تي-شيرت

٦ طماطم ٧ طبلة ٨ منجة ٩ سلّة ١٠ قلادة

Activity 4

١ سوقان/ين ٢ طبقان/ين ٣ سلّتان/ين ٤ كيسان/ين

٥ قميصان/ين ٦ خاتمان/ين ٧ طبلتان/ين

٨ حقيبتان/ين ٩ قلمان/ين ١٠ قلادتان/ين

Activity 5

– أهلاً. صباح الخير!

– صباح النور. هل عِندَكُم صَنادِل؟

– نعم. عِندَنا هذا الصَندَل الجديد.

– لا، أريد صندل جلد من فضلك.

– صندل جلد؟ الصندل الأبيَض جميل.

– نعم، جميل. بكم هذا، من فضلك؟

– بعشرة جنيهات.

– تفضّل. عشرة جنيهات.

– شكراً، مع السلامة.

Activity 6

١ بكم الطبلة؟ ٢ بكم كيلو التفّاح؟

٣ القلادة بعشرة جنيهات. ٤ السلّة بسبعة جنيهات.

٥ كيلو الطماطم بثلاثة جنيهات. ٦ بكم الطبق النُحاس؟

٧ الصندل الجلد بثمانية جنيهات.

Activity 7

أنت: هل عندكم برتقال؟ hal ɛindakum burtuqāl?

أنت: كيلو برتقال مصريّ من فضلك.
kīlū burtuqāl miṣrīy min faḍlak.

أنت: وبكم البطاطس؟ wa-bikam al-baṭāṭis?

أنت: ثلاثة كيلو من فضلك. بكم هذا؟
thalātha kīlū min faḍlak. bikam hādhā?

أنت: تفضّل. هل عندك كيس؟ tafaḍḍal. hal ɛindak kīs?

unit 11 Plurals and colours

Activity 1

Plural	Meaning	Root letters	Word
أقلام	pen	ق/ل/م	قلَم
أطباق	plate	ط/ب/ق	طبَق
قلوب	heart	ق/ل/ب	قلب
مدرّسون	teacher	د/ر/س	مُدَرِّس
أسعار	price	س/ع/ر	سِعر
سيّارات	car	س/ي/ر	سيّارة
سيوف	sword	س/ي/ف	سَيف
أولاد	boy	و/ل/د	وَلَد
ألوان	colour	ل/و/ن	لَون
حفلات	party	ح/ف/ل	حَفلة
أكواب	glass/tumbler	ك/و/ب	كوب
شموع	candle	ش/م/ع	شَمعة
مصوّرون	photographer	ص/و/ر	مُصَوِّر
أكياس	bag	ك/ي/س	كيس
ممرّضات	nurse	م/ر/ض	مُمَرِّضة

Activity 2

١ هذه هي أقلامي. ٢ هذه هي أكوابي ٣ هذا هو كوبي.

٤ هذه هي أطباقي. ٥ هذه هي سيّارتي. ٦ هذه هي سيوفي.

٧ هؤلاء هم أولادي. ٨ هذه هي حقيبتي.

٩ هذا هو مفتاحي. ١٠ هذه هي شموعي.

Activity 3

هذا بَيت.

You should have revealed a blue sky and a yellow house with a garden, two windows, a black door and a red roof.

Activity 4

Who?	Item(s)	Description
Dad	shirt	white (cotton) for parties
Tariq	bag	black leather for school
Randa	pens	for writing (red and black)
Adil	tent	blue (lightweight)
Mum	movies	old French
Nunu	sandals	small plastic (green)
Mimi	hat	yellow (cotton or silk)

Activity 5

أنت: أريد تي–شيرت قطن. urīd tī-shīrt quṭn.

أنت: أفضّل الأزرق. ufaḍḍil al-azraq.

أنت: وهل عندكم قبّعات قطن؟
wa-hal ɛindakum qubbaɛāt quṭn?

أنت: القبعة البيضاء. al-qubbaɛa al-bayḍā'.

أنت: تفضّل. شكراً. tafaḍḍal. shukran.

unit 12 Eating and drinking

Activity 1

ل	ا	ق	ت	ر	ب	ث	ف	ز	ك	س	ع
ح	ن	ب	ي	ه	ة	م	ع	ط	م	ا	س
م	خ	س	م	ص	ي	ا	ن	و	ك	ظ	ي
ا	ر	ك	س	ا	ش	ض	ل	ز	ر	أ	ر
ة	ظ	و	م	ج	ا	ج	د	ج	و	ل	ح
ؤ	ل	ي	ص	ش	ي	ه	د	ة	ن	ب	ج
ن	ي	ت	ا	ي	ذ	ص	ر	غ	ة	ف	ع
ة	ز	ع	ط	س	ج	ك	م	س	ك	ي	ب
ز	و	م	ذ	خ	ر	و	د	م	و	ث	ي
ي	ة	ض	ي	ب	ي	ل	ح	غ	ا	ن	ض
ت	ز	ب	ق	ز	ك	ا	ن	ي	ط	ب	ك
ل	ا	ق	ب	ه	ذ	ح	ة	ر	ي	ص	ع

Activity 2

١ كيس ٢ كيلو ٣ قطعة ٤ علبة ٥ علبة
٦ نصف لتر ٧ زجاجة ٨ لتر ٩ ربع كيلو ١٠ أنبوبة

Activity 3

بسكويت/زجاجة أسنان/مسحوق
برتقال/جبنة مسحوق/أسنان
كيس/تفّاح مسحوق

Jamila didn't buy the toothpaste. The bill was 45 pounds.

Activity 4

١ ✗ ٢ ✓ ٣ ✓ ٤ ✓ ٥ ✗
٦ ✗ ٧ ✓ ٨ ✓ ٩ ✗ ١٠ ✓

Activity 5

How you fill the gaps depends on your personal preferences. Try to check your answer with an Arabic speaker.

Activity 6

أنت: يا جرسون! من فضلك. yā garsūn! min faḍlak.

أنت: آخذ دجاج مشويّ بالأرزّ. ākhudh dajāj mashwī bil-aruzz.

أنت: وأريد سلطة الطماطم. wa-urīd salaṭa biṭ-ṭamāṭim.

أنت: آخذ عصير برتقال بارد. ākhudh ɛaṣīr burtuqāl bārid.

أنت: نعم. آيس كويم بالفواكه من فضلك.
naɛam. āyis krīm bil-fawākih, min faḍlak.

unit 13 What happened yesterday

Activity 1

١d, ٢h, ٣j, ٤a, ٥g, ٦i, ٧b, ٨c, ٩f, ١٠e

Activity 2

١ شربتُ فنجان شاي. ٢ أكلتُ دجاجة/دجاجاً.
٣ جلستُ على كرسيّ. ٤ كتبتُ خطاباً/خطابات.
٥ ذهبتُ إلى البنك. ٦ رجعتُ إلى البيت.
٧ وجدتُ المفتاح في حقيبتي. ٨ فتحتُ الباب مع مفتاحي.

Activity 3

١ ذَهَبْتَ ٢ شَرِبْتُ ٣ كَتَبَ ٤ فَتَحْتَ ٥ أكَلْتِ
٦ وَجَدْتَ ٧ خَرَجَ ٨ جَلَسْتِ ٩ سَمِعْتَ ١٠ فَعَلْتُ

Activity 4

NAME	OCCUPATION	YESTERDAY			
		Did what daytime?	Did what evening?	Ate what?	Drank what?
Waheed	newspaper journalist	went to office wrote about theft	sat with wife	fish	coffee
Mary	nurse	went to hospital went to market	wrote a letter to sister	egg salad	tea
Warda	pupil	went to school went to friend's house	watched TV	pizza and chips	cola

Activity 5

1 In the south of Lebanon. **2** By bus. **3** The old city. **4** Three. **5** Gold, carpenters' and fishmongers' markets. **6** Old yellow houses. **7** A Lebanese restaurant. **8** Falafel, labna (yoghurt dip), coffee. **9** In the evening. **10** 'What did you do yesterday?'

Activity 6

خَرَجَ يوسف أمس صباحاً وذَهَبَ بالباص إلى صَيدا، وهي مدينة جميلة في جنوب لبنان.

أوّلاً ذَهَبَ إلى المدينة القديمة ووَجَدَ أسواق الذهب والنَجّارين والسَمّاكين وبيوتاً قديمة صَفراء. بعد ذلك ذَهَبَ إلى مطعم لبنانيّ و أَكَلَ فَلافِل ولَبنة وشَرِبَ قهوة عربيّة. أخيراً رَجَعَ إلى بيروت مساءً.

Activity 7

أنت: ذهبتُ إلى سوق الذهب. dhahabtu ilā sūq adh-dhahab.

أنت: وجدتُ قلادة لأختي. wajadtu qilāda li-ukhtī.

أنت: أكلتُ في مطعم لبنانيّ. alkaltu fī maṭɛam lubnānīy.

أنت: شربتُ قهوة عربيّة. sharibtu qahwa ɛarabīyya.

أنت: لا. كتبتُ إيميل لأصحابي. lā. katabtu īmayl li-aṣḥābī.

unit 14 Wish you were here

Activity 1

Plural	Meaning	Root letters	Word
كِلاب	dog	ك/ل/ب	كَلب
رِجال	man	ر/ج/ل	رَجُل
صُوَر	picture	ص/و/ر	صورة
جِبال	mountain	ج/ب/ل	جبَل
لُعَب	game	ل/ع/ب	لُعبة
غُرَف	room	غ/ر/ف	غُرفة
بِحار	sea	ب/ح/ر	بَحر
جِمال	camel	ج/م/ل	جَمَل
عُلَب	box	ع/ل/ب	عُلبة

Activity 2

f, m, b, h, k, c, i, g, n, a, l, j, d, e

Activity 3

وجدنا سبعة جِمال. وجدنا ثلاث سيّارات.

وجدنا أربع درّاجات. وجدنا ثلاث وثلاثين عُلبة.

وجدنا عشر صُوَر. وجدنا خمسة عشر شَيخاً.

وجدنا ستّة كِلاب. وجدنا خمسين طَبلة.

وجدنا عشرين طبَقاً. وجدنا ست وثمانين لُعبة.

وجدنا أربعة عشر حِماراً. وجدنا تسعة أولاد.

Activity 4

١ تونس ٢ حارّ ٣ ٤٠ ٤ البحر

٥ القلعة ٦ سمكاً ٧ السوق ٨ الفندق

Activity 5

١ عزيزتي صفاء ٢ مُشمس وحارّ جدّاً ٣ في الشمال الشرقي

٤ شجر وجبال ٥ أنا والأولاد ٦ القَلعة القديمة

٧ سمك بالكُسكُس ٨ مع تَحياتي

Activity 6

أنت: نحن في مدينة أفينيون. naḥnu fī madīnat afīnyūn.

أنت: ممطر وبارد. درجة الحرارة ١٥.

mumṭir wa-bārid. darajat al-ḥarāra khamsat ɛashar.

أنت: لا، وجدنا بيتاً في المدينة القديمة.

la, wajadnā bayt(an) fīl-madīna al-qadīma.

أنت: أمس ذهبنا إلى القصر القديم ... وجلسنا بجانب النهر.

ams dhahabnā ilā l-qaṣr al-qadīm … wa-jalasnā bijānib an-nahr.

أنت: ماذا فعلت أمس يا تامر؟ mādhā faɛalta ams yā tāmir?

unit 15 Review

Activity 1

في الشبّاك هناك خمسة جمال، خمسة عشر كلباً، ثلاثة عشر كتاباً، سبعة أقلام، ستّة قُلوب، ثلاث درّاجات، ستّة عشر سَيفاً، ثلاثة تليفونات، أربع سيّارات، أربعة عشر شمعة.

Activity 2

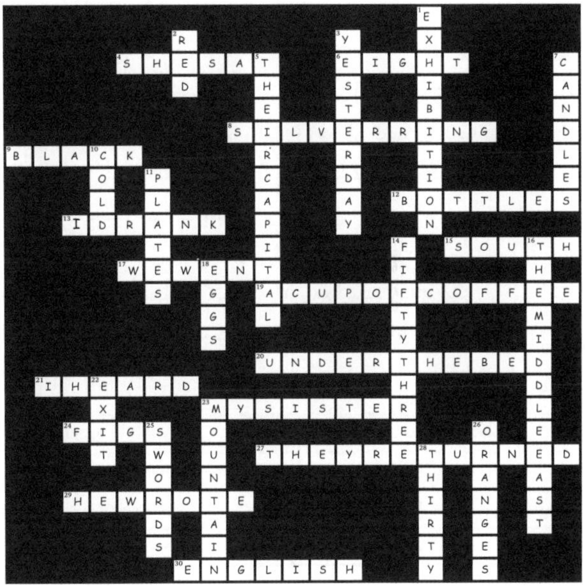

Activity 3

١f, ٢g, ٣h, ٤e, ٥c, ٦d, ٧b, ٨a

Activity 4

Free writing. *Try to show your postcard to an Arabic-speaking teacher or friend.*

Activity 5

١ وجدتُ المفتاح تحت الكرسيّ. ٢ الطقس حارّ جدّاً اليوم.
٣ شربنا قهوة في السوق. ٤ هل ذهبتُم إلى المتحف؟ ٥ نزلوا في فندق صغير. ٦ جلستُ على الكرسيّ الأسود بجانب الباب.

Activity 6

أنت: هل وجدتِ حقيبتك؟ hal wajadti ḥaqībatik?

أنت: أين ذهبتِ أمس؟ ayna dhahabti ams?

أنت: أين جلستِ في المطعم؟ ayna jalasti fil-maṭɛam?

أنت: وكيف رجعتِ إلى البيت؟ wa-kayfa rajaɛti ilā l-bayt?

أنت: آه... هل حقيبتك سوداء؟ āh… hal ḥaqībatik sawdā'?

أنت: نعم، بين مقعدي والباب! naɛam, bayna miqɛadī wal-bāb!

unit 16 Every day

Activity 1

١ الساعة الثالثة	٢ الساعة الخامِسة
٣ الساعة السابِعة	٤ الساعة الرابِعة
٥ الساعة السادِسة والنِصف	٦ الساعة العاشِرة والنِصف
٧ الساعة التاسِعة والرُبع	٨ الساعة الواحِدة والرُبع
٩ الساعة الثامِنة إلا رُبعاً	١٠ الساعة الخامِسة إلا ثُلثاً

Activity 2

سامي مهندس ميكانيكيّ. كلّ يوم يَغسِل وَجهَهُ الساعة السادسة ويَلبِس مَلابِس العمل، ثُمّ يَأكُل الإفطار الساعة السادسة والنصف. عادةً يَخرُج من البيت الساعة السابعة ويَذهَب إلى مَصنَع السيّارات بالقطار. يَرجِع من المصنع إلى البيت الساعة الرابعة والرُّبع ويَرسُم صُوَراً للشَّجَر والجِبال والأنهار بالألوان. يأكل العَشاء الساعة الثامنة إلا ربعاً وبعد ذلك يَشرَب فنجان شاي. أخيراً يَلبِس البيجاما ويَنام الساعة العاشرة.

Activity 3

	wake up	تَصحو الساعة السادسة
	put on school clothes	تَلبَس ملابس المدرسة
	eat breakfast	تَأكُل الإفطار الساذسة والنصف
	leave house	تَخرُج من البيت السابعة والرُّبع
	go to school by bicycle	تَذهَب إلى المدرسة بالدرّاجة
	return from school	تَرجِع من المدرسة الساعة الثالثة
	school work ('write lessons') play with little sister	تَكتُب دروسها وتلعَب مع أُختها
	eat dinner	تَأكُل العشاء الساعة الثامنة
	drink glass milk	تَشرَب كوب حليب
	put on pyjamas	تَلبَس البيجاما التاسعة إلا رُبعاً
	sleep	تَنام التاسعة والثُّلث

Activity 4

أنا تلميذة في المدرسة. كلّ يوم أَصحو الساعة السادسة وأَلبِس مَلابِسِ المدرسة، ثُمّ آكُل الإفطار الساعة السادسة والنصف. عادةً أَخرُج من البيت الساعة السابعة والرُّبع وأَذهَب إلى المدرسة بالدرّاجة. أَرجِع من المدرسة إلى البيت الساعة الثالثة. بعد ذلك عادةً أَكتُب دروسي وأَلعَب مع أُختي. آكل العَشاء الساعة الثامنة وبعد ذلك أَشرَب كوب حليب. أخيراً أَلبس البيجاما الساعة التاسعة إلا ربعاً وأَنام التاسعة والثُّلث.

Activity 5

١ تَذهَب	٢ أَشرَب	٣ يدرُسون	٤ نَغسِل
٥ تَأكُلين	٦ تَلعَب	٧ تَلبَسون	٨ يَكتُبون

تلبَسون؛ نغسِل؛ أشرَب؛ يدرُسون؛ تلعَب

Activity 6

أنت: عادةً نأكل الإفطار الساعة الثامنة ...

ʿādatan na'kul al-ifṭār as-sāʿa ath-thāmina ...

وأخرج من البيت الثامنة والنصف.

w-akhruj min al-bayt ath-thāmina wan-niṣf.

أنت: أذهب إلى وسط المدينة بالقطار ...

adh-hab ilā wasaṭ al-madīna bil-qiṭār ...

ثمّ أذهب بالأتوبيس (بالباص) إلى المكتب.

thumma adh-hab bil-utūbīs (bil-bāṣ) ilā l-maktab.

أنت: أرجع الساعة الخامسة والنصف أو السادسة إلا ربعاً ...

arjaʿ as-sāʿa al-khāmisa wan-niṣf aw as-sādisa ilā rubʿan ...

ونأكل العشاء الساعة السابعة والنصف.

wa-na'kul al-ʿashā' as-sāʿa as-sābiʿa wan-niṣf.

wa-anta? mādhā tafʿal kull yawm? وأنت؟ ماذا تفعل كلّ اليوم؟

unit 17 Comparing things

Activity 1

Meaning	Comparative	Root letters	Adjective
bigger/larger	أكبَر	ك/ب/ر	كبير
smaller	أصغَر	ص/غ/ر	صغير
more beautiful	أجمَل	ج/م/ل	جميل
cheaper	أرخَص	ر/خ/ص	رخيص
colder	أبرَد	ب/ر/د	بارد
shorter	أقصَر	ق/ص/ر	قصير
happier	أسعَد	س/ع/د	سَعيد
faster	أسرَع	س/ر/ع	سريع
heavier	أثقَل	ث/ق/ل	ثقيل
newer	أجَدّ	ج/د/د	جديد
lighter	أخَفّ	خ/ف/ف	خفيف
richer	أغنَى	غ/ن/ي	غَنيّ
more important	أهَمّ	ه/م/م	هامّ
stronger	أقوَى	ق/و/ي	قَويّ
sweeter	أحلَى	ح/ل/و	حُلو

Activity 2

بيتي أكبر من بيتك. هو أكبر بيت في الشارع!

ابني أطول من ابنك. هو أطول ولد في الشارع!

بنتي أجمل من بنتك. هي أجمل بنت في الشارع!

خاتمي أقدم من خاتمك. هو أقدم خاتم في الشارع!

سيّارتي أسرع من سيّارتك. هي أسرع سيّارة في الشارع!

درّاجتي أجدّ من درّاجتك. هي أجدّ درّاجة في الشارع!

حقيبتي أخفّ من حقيبتك. هي أخفّ حقيبة في الشارع!

عصيري أحلى من عصيرك. هو أحلى عصير في الشارع!

زوجي أغنى من زوجك. هو أغنى رجل في الشارع!

قلادتي أغلى من قلادتك. هي أغلى قلادة في الشارع!

Activity 3

١ يوم السبت ٢ يوم الأحد ٣ يوم الاثنين ٤ يوم الثلاثاء
٥ يوم الأربعاء ٦ يوم الخميس ٧ يوم الجمعة

Activity 4

يوم الأسبوع	الصورة	ماذا فعل طارق؟
الثلاثاء	٢	يطبُخ السمك للعَشاء.
الأربعاء	٥	يأكل في مطعم إيرانيّ.
الخميس	٧	يذهَب إلى البنك.
السبت	٦	يكتُب إيميل لابن أخته.
الجمعة	٣	يشرَب قهوة في بيت صاحبه.
الأحد	٤	يلعَب مع الكلب خارج المدينة.
الاثنين	١	يجلِس مع أمّه في بيتها.

Activity 5

يوم الأحد عادةً ألعَب مع الكلب خارج المدينة.
يوم الاثنين عادةً أجلِس مع أمّي في بيتها.
يوم الثلاثاء عادةً أطبُخ السمك للعَشاء.
يوم الأربعاء عادةً آكُل في مطعم إيرانيّ.
يوم الخميس عادةً أذهَب إلى البنك.
يوم الجمعة عادةً أشرَب قهوة في بيت صاحبي.
يوم السبت عادةً أكتُب إيميل لابن أختي.

Activity 6

١ كُنتُ في البنك.
٢ كانوا في المصنع.
٣ كانَت طبّاخة.
٤ هل كُنتَ الأطول؟
٥ كان ممثّلاً.
٦ كانَت الغرفة جميلة.
٧ كُنّا فقراء.
٨ هل كُنتِ سعيدة؟
٩ كانَت الأطباق جديدة.
١٠ هل كُنتُم أصحاباً؟

Activity 7

أنت: هذا جدّي. hādhā jaddī.
أنت: منذ أربعين سنة كان ممثّلاً.
mundhu arbaعīn sana kāna mumaththil(an).
أنت:نعم. كان ممثّلاً شهيراً. naعam. kāna mumaththil(an) shahīr(an).
كان أغنى رجل في المدينة! kāna aghnā rajul fil-madīna!
أنت: كانت أفضل طبّاخة! kānat afḍal ṭabbākha!
كانت حلوياتها شهيّة. kānat ḥalawīyyāt(u)hā shahīyyā.
أنت: كنتُ أسعد طفل في الشارع! kuntu asعad ṭifl fīsh-shāriع!

unit 18 Education and business

Activity 1

١e, ٢a, ٣i, ٤k, ٥j, ٦m, ٧l, ٨f, ٩n, ١٠h, ١١g, ١٢c, ١٣b, ١٤d

Activity 2

١ يدرُسون الجغرافيا من الساعة التاسعة حتّى العاشرة إلا ربعاً.
٢ يدرُسون العربيّة من الساعة العاشرة إلا ربعاً حتّى الحادية عشرة.
٣ يدرُسون الكيمياء من الساعة الحادية عشرة حتّى الثانية عشرة والنصف.
٤ يأكُلون الغداء من الساعة الثانية عشرة والنصف حتّى الثانية والربع.
٥ يدرُسون الرياضيّات من الساعة الثانية والربع حتّى الساعة الثالثة.
٦ يدرُسون الموسيقى من الساعة الثالثة حتّى الرابعة إلا ربعاً.

Activity 3

Plural فعلاء	Person فعيل	Noun فعالة	Root letters
سُفَراء ambassadors	سَفير ambassador	سِفارة embassy	س/ف/ر
وُزَراء ministers	وَزير minister	وِزارة ministry	و/ز/ر
وُكَلاء agents	وَكيل agent	وَكالة agency	و/ك/ل
زُعَماء leaders	زَعيم leader	زَعامة leadership	ز/ع/م
رُؤَساء presidents	رَئيس president	رِئاسة presidency	ر/ء/س
أُمَراء princes/emirs	أمير prince/emir	إمارة emirate	ء/م/ر
زُمَلاء colleagues	زَميل colleague	زَمالة colleagueship	ز/م/ل

Activity 4

ا ج ت م ا ع
و ك ا ل ة
س ف ا ر ة
ش ر ك ة
م ع ر ض
م ؤ ت م ر
م ج ل س

Additional vocabulary:
جلسة عمَل *(workshop)*

Activity 5

١d, ٢g, ٣a, ٤i, ٥h, ٦j, ٧b, ٨f, ٩e, ١٠c

Activity 6

١ هاشم ٢ اليوم ٣ اسمها ٤ المستشفى ٥ السادسة
٦ هامّة ٧ ابن ٨ يعمل ٩ قال ١٠ الصفراء

Activity 7

١ رجعتُ من الإمارات يوم الجمعة.
٢ ندرُس العربيّة في الجامعة.
٣ سميرة هي رَئيسة الشركة.
٤ كلّ يوم أربعاء تَحْضُر اجتماعاً مع وَكالة الإعلان.
٥ لا أُحبّ الرياضيّات أو العُلوم.
٦ أُفَضِّل التاريخ واللُّغات.

Activity 8

أنت: ذهبتُ إلى وزارة الصناعة. dhahabtu ilā wizārat al-ṣināعa.
أنت: حضرتُ مؤتمراً كبيراً. ḥaḍartu mu'tamar(an) kabīr(an).
أنت: مع مهندسين من الشرق الأوسط.
maعa muhandisīn min ash-sharq al-awsaṭ.
أنت: حضر رئيس الوزراء. ḥaḍara ra'īs al-wuzarā.
أنت: نعم وجلستُ بجانبه! naعam, wa-jalastu bi-jānibihi!

unit 19 Future plans

Activity 1

١ يناير ٢ فبراير ٣ مارس ٤ أبريل
٥ مايو ٦ يونيو ٧ يوليو ٨ أغسطس
٩ سبتمبر ١٠ أكتوبر ١١ نوفمبر ١٢ ديسمبر

Activity 2

١ يوم الخميس، ١٥ يناير ٢ يوم الجمعة ٢٠ مارس
٣ يوم الإثنين ٩ سبتمبر ٤ يوم الثلاثاء ٢٢ يونيو
٥ يوم الأحد ١٤ فبراير ٦ يوم الخميس ٣ أبريل
٧ يوم الأربعاء ١٢ يوليو ٨ يوم السبت ٣١ أغسطس

Activity 3

Breakfast at 5:20AM; Leave hotel at 6am; Visits: 1 Valley of the Kings, 2 Pharaonic Museum, *(*Lunch: Amun Restaurant), 3 Karnak Temple; Return to hotel 8PM

Activity 4

١ سَتَزور أمّها في المستشفى الساعة التاسعة والنصف.
٢ سَتَحضُر اجتماعاً في المدرسة الساعة الحادية عشرة والثُلث.
٣ سَتَأكُل الغداء مع منيرة الساعة الواحدة (بعد الظُهر).
٤ سَتذهَب إلى البقّال الساعة الثانية والربع (بعد الظُهر).
٥ سَتكتُب إيميل للبنك الساعة الرابعة (بعد الظُهر).
٦ سَتغسِل الملابس الساعة الخامسة (بعد الظُهر).
٧ سَتَطبُخ اللحم للعشاء الساعة السادسة والنصف (مساءً).

Activity 5

١ سَيَحضُر ٢ سَأرجِع ٣ سَيَدرُس ٤ سَنُقابِل
٥ سَتَأكُل ٦ سَأُسافِر ٧ سَيَذهَب/سَيَزورون ٨ سَتَطيرين

Activity 6

Free writing. *Try to show to an Arabic speaker.*

Activity 7

أنت: غداً سنذهب إلى الأقصر بالقطار.
ghadan sa-nadh-hab ilā l-aqṣur bil-qiṭār
أنت: نعم. سنسافر لتسع ساعات. naᶜam. sa-nusāfir li-tisᶜ sāᶜāt.
أنت: سننام في القطار. sa-nanām fīl-qiṭār.
أنت: السبت سنزور وادي الملوك. as-sabt sa-nazūr wādī al-mulūk.
وسنذهب إلى معبد الكرنك (يوم) الأحد.
wa sa-nadh-hab ilā maᶜbad al-karnak (yawm) al-aḥad.

unit 20 Review

Activity 1

١ أمس رَجَعوا الساعة الرابعة.
٢ في المستقبل سَأدرُس العربيّة.
٣ منذُ عشرين سنة كان رجلاً فقيراً.
٤ سَنَبدَأ الدِراسة بَعدَ شهرَين.
٥ هل جلستَ مع جَدّك أمس؟
٦ أين ستُقابِلين زينة غداً؟
٧ عادةً تُسافر الوزيرة بالقطار.
٨ مُنذُ أسبوع حَضَر مُؤتَمراً.

Activity 2

١ ليس عندنا... ٢ لا أشرب... ٣ لم تَذهَب... ٤ ليس لي...
٥ ليس هناك... ٦ لا نسمع... ٧ لم نُجرِّب... ٨ لم تُسافِروا

Activity 3

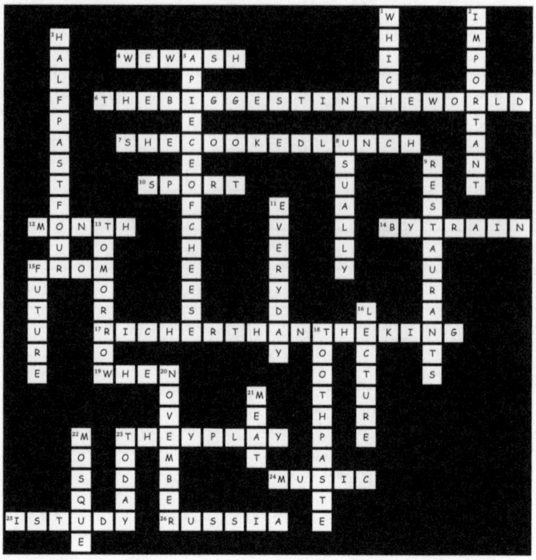

Activity 4

1 Baker, every day 4AM–7PM. 2 Two. 3 Thursday, Friday and Saturday. 4 They were poor, but now he's the richest man in town. 5 90 bakeries in the Middle East. 6 In a large beautiful palace beside the river with his wife and children. 7 Yes, he was happy; his father was strong and taught him the love of work; his mother was generous/beautiful/the best cook in the street. 8 He eats warm bread and a piece of cheese for breakfast.

Activity 5

١ مَخبَز/مَخابِز ٢ للوالدين ٣ ولذلك ٤ والده ٥ يَعيش
٦ كُنتُ سَعيداً ٧ حُبّ العَمَل ٨ خُبز دافِئ ٩ أشهَر ١٠ إلى اليوم

Activity 6

١ تَلعَب جميلة كرة الريشة في النادي.
٢ عادةً أصحو الساعة السابعة والنصف.
٣ نأكُل الفواكه كلّ يوم.
٤ النيل هو أطول نهر في العالم.
٥ سأكتُب لك إيميل غداً.
٦ كيف سَيُسافِرون إلى الأقصر؟

Activity 7

أنت: رجعنا من الأقصر الإثنين. rajaᶜnā min al-aqṣur al-ithnayn.
وأمس زرنا الأزهر. wa-ams zurna al-azhar.
هو أقدم جامعة في العالم. huwa aqdam jāmiᶜa fīl-ᶜālam.
أنت: ثمّ أكلنا حمام بالخبز العربيّ. كان شهيّاً!
thumma akalnā ḥamām bil-khubz al-ᶜarabī. kāna shahīyyan!
أنت: ستقلع طائرتنا غداً الساعة الثالثة صباحاً.
sa-tuqliᶜ ṭā'irat(u)nā ghadan as-sāᶜa ath-thālitha ṣabāḥan.
أنت: فسأقول مع السلامة الآن. fa sa-aqūl "maᶜa s-salāma" al-ān.
ولكني سأدرس العربيّة كلّ يوم.
wa-lākinnī sa-adrus al-ᶜarabīyya kull yawm.
أعرف أفضل كتاب في العالم! aᶜrif afḍal kitāb fīl-ᶜālam!